Basic

GLOBAL GATE
— Video-based Four Skills Training —

Shoma Aota   Ayaka Koshiishi   Bill Benfield   Akira Morita

SEIBIDO

photographs by

iStockphoto / Shutterstock / Getty Images

時事 / dpa/時事通信フォト

videos by

Ready to Run

StreamLine

Web 動画・音声ファイルのストリーミング再生について

CD マーク及び Web 動画マークがある箇所は、PC、スマートフォン、タブレット端末において、無料でストリーミング再生することができます。下記 URL よりご利用ください。再生手順や動作環境などは本書巻末の「Web 動画のご案内」をご覧ください。

https://st.seibido.co.jp

音声ファイルのダウンロードについて

CD マークがある箇所は、ダウンロードすることも可能です。下記 URL の書籍詳細ページにあるダウンロードアイコンをクリックしてください。

https://www.seibido.co.jp/ad685

Global Gate Basic

CONTENTS

LEARNING OVERVIEW

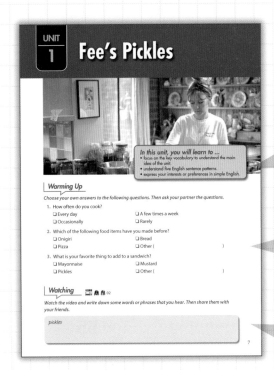

In this unit, you will learn to ...

An overview of the unit helps students focus on learning outcomes.

Warming Up

Activates students' background knowledge of the topic.

Watching

Presents a video for students to watch and recognize the words they hear.

Vocabulary

Teaches the definition and usage of the topic-related words or phrases.

Tips on Listening and Speaking

Presents useful information for listening and speaking.

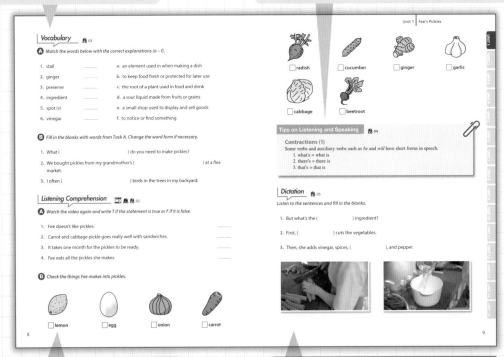

Listening Comprehension

Presents various review questions for students to check comprehension.

Dictation

Teaches sound features related to Tips on Listening and Speaking as well as content words from the video.

Retelling

Presents part of the video for students to watch and retell in their own words.

Grammar

Presents images or graphical explanations of the grammar point of the unit.

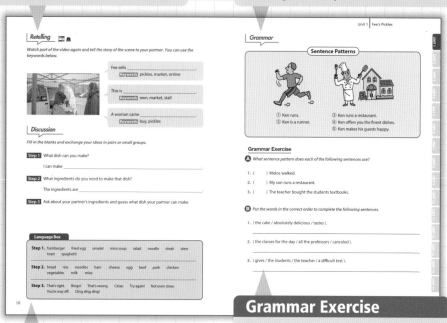

Discussion

Presents step-by-step exercises to enhance students' critical thinking skills.

Grammar Exercise

Enhances students' grammar ability through a variety of exercises.

Vocabulary Check

Teaches useful vocabulary from the Reading.

Reading

Features an interesting article related to the topic of the video.

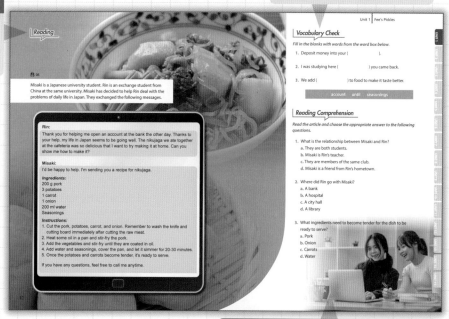

Reading Comprehension

Presents multiple-choice questions for students to check comprehension.

LEARNING OVERVIEW

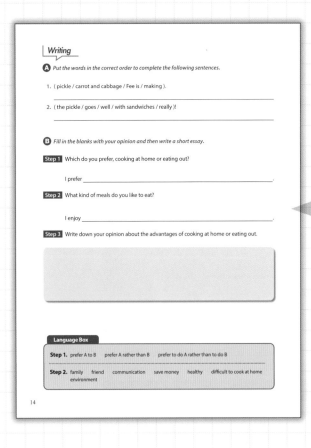

Writing

Presents step-by-step exercises to aid output of students' ideas or opinions.

Useful Expressions for Discussions

Presents useful expressions for each discussion exercise.

Useful Expressions for Discussions

Giving your thoughts/opinions

☐ I believe that it is a good idea (to do something) because …
☐ I don't think that it is a good idea (that we send it to them) because …
☐ In my opinion, it is not important (to do something) because …
☐ My opinion is (that we should look after them) because …
☐ It was interesting to know that …
☐ I was surprised [at / by] the fact that …
☐ The most interesting finding is that …

Agreeing

☐ I agree with [you / your idea].
☐ I think so, too.
☐ I suppose you're right.
☐ I feel the same way.
☐ I have no objections.
☐ That's a good idea.

Disagreeing

☐ I disagree with [you / your idea].
☐ I don't think so.
☐ I have a different opinion.
☐ I'm against it.
☐ That's a good opinion, but …
☐ That can be true, but …

Listing / Ordering

☐ A is more important than B in terms of …
☐ A is followed by B.
☐ A is one of the most important items because …
☐ The most important point here is that …
☐ We should focus on importance first. Then …
☐ The first point is … The second point is …
☐ First, … [Second / Then], … [Lastly / Finally], …

Categorizing

☐ They can be classified into …
☐ A belongs to B in that …
☐ A is included in B
☐ There are [two / three / four] kinds of …

Making suggestions/evaluation

☐ It is suggested that …
☐ I would suggest that …
☐ It was [excellent > great > good > fair > poor > bad].
☐ More attention should be given to …
☐ You should have paid attention to …
☐ You had better do.

In this unit, you will learn to ...
- focus on the key vocabulary to understand the main idea of the unit.
- understand five English sentence patterns.
- express your interests or preferences in simple English.

Warming Up

Choose your own answers to the following questions. Then ask your partner the questions.

1. How often do you cook?
   - ❏ Every day
   - ❏ A few times a week
   - ❏ Occasionally
   - ❏ Rarely

2. Which of the following food items have you made before?
   - ❏ Onigiri
   - ❏ Bread
   - ❏ Pizza
   - ❏ Other (   )

3. What is your favorite thing to add to a sandwich?
   - ❏ Mayonnaise
   - ❏ Mustard
   - ❏ Pickles
   - ❏ Other (   )

Watching 　WEB動画 🖥 📀 DVD 📀 CD 02

Watch the video and write down some words or phrases that you hear. Then share them with your friends.

pickles

Vocabulary 🎧 03

A *Match the words below with the correct explanations (a – f).*

1. stall   _____   **a.** an element used in when making a dish

2. ginger   _____   **b.** to keep food fresh or protected for later use

3. preserve   _____   **c.** the root of a plant used in food and drink

4. ingredient   _____   **d.** a sour liquid made from fruits or grains

5. spot (v)   _____   **e.** a small shop used to display and sell goods

6. vinegar   _____   **f.** to notice or find something

B *Fill in the blanks with words from Task A. Change the word form if necessary.*

1. What (   ) do you need to make pickles?

2. We bought pickles from my grandmother's (   ) at a flea market.

3. I often (   ) birds in the trees in my backyard.

Listening Comprehension 📺WEB動画 📀DVD 🎧02

A *Watch the video again and write T if the statement is true or F if it is false.*

1. Fee doesn't like pickles.   _____

2. Carrot and cabbage pickle goes really well with sandwiches.   _____

3. It takes one month for the pickles to be ready.   _____

4. Fee eats all the pickles she makes.   _____

B *Check the things Fee makes into pickles.*

☐ lemon   ☐ egg   ☐ onion   ☐ carrot

☐ radish   ☐ cucumber   ☐ ginger   ☐ garlic

☐ cabbage   ☐ beetroot

Tips on Listening and Speaking   🎵 04

Contractions (1)
Some verbs and auxiliary verbs such as *be* and *will* have short forms in speech.
  1. what's = what is
  2. there's = there is
  3. that's = that is

Dictation   🎵 05

Listen to the sentences and fill in the blanks.

1. But what's the (   ) ingredient?

2. First, (   ) cuts the vegetables.

3. Then, she adds vinegar, spices, (   ), and pepper.

Retelling

WEB動画 📺 💿DVD

Watch part of the video again and tell the story of the scene to your partner. You can use the keywords below.

Fee sells _____.
Keywords pickles, market, online

This is _____.
Keywords own, market, stall

A woman came _____.
Keywords buy, pickles

Discussion

Fill in the blanks and exchange your ideas in pairs or small groups.

Step 1 What dish can you make?

I can make _____.

Step 2 What ingredients do you need to make that dish?

The ingredients are _____.

Step 3 Ask about your partner's ingredients and guess what dish your partner can make.

Language Box

Step 1. hamburger   fried egg   omelet   miso soup   salad   noodle   steak   stew
toast   spaghetti

....

Step 2. bread   rice   noodles   ham   cheese   egg   beef   pork   chicken
vegetables   milk   miso

....

Step 3. That's right.   Bingo!   That's wrong.   Close.   Try again!   Not even close.
You're way off.   Ding ding ding!

Grammar

Sentence Patterns

① Ken runs.
② Ken is a runner.

③ Ken runs a restaurant.
④ Ken offers you the finest dishes.
⑤ Ken makes his guests happy.

Grammar Exercise

A *What sentence pattern does each of the following sentences use?*

1. (   ) Melos walked.

2. (   ) My son runs a restaurant.

3. (   ) The teacher bought the students textbooks.

B *Put the words in the correct order to complete the following sentences.*

1. (the cake / absolutely delicious / tastes).

   _____

2. (the classes for the day / all the professors / canceled).

   _____

3. (gives / the students / the teacher / a difficult test).

   _____

11

06

Misaki is a Japanese university student. Rin is an exchange student from China at the same university. Misaki has decided to help Rin deal with the problems of daily life in Japan. They exchanged the following messages.

Rin:

Thank you for helping me open an account at the bank the other day. Thanks to your help, my life in Japan seems to be going well. The nikujaga we ate together at the cafeteria was so delicious that I want to try making it at home. Can you show me how to make it?

Misaki:

I'd be happy to help. I'm sending you a recipe for nikujaga.

Ingredients:
200 g pork
3 potatoes
1 carrot
1 onion
200 ml water
Seasonings

Instructions:
1. Cut the pork, potatoes, carrot, and onion. Remember to wash the knife and cutting board immediately after cutting the raw meat.
2. Heat some oil in a pan and stir-fry the pork.
3. Add the vegetables and stir-fry until they are coated in oil.
4. Add water and seasonings, cover the pan, and let it simmer for 20-30 minutes.
5. Once the potatoes and carrots become tender, it's ready to serve.

If you have any questions, feel free to call me anytime.

Vocabulary Check

Fill in the blanks with words from the word box below.

1. Deposit money into your (   ).

2. I was studying here (   ) you came back.

3. We add (   ) to food to make it taste better.

| account | until | seasonings |

Reading Comprehension

Read the article and choose the appropriate answer to the following questions.

1. What is the relationship between Misaki and Rin?
   a. They are both students.
   b. Misaki is Rin's teacher.
   c. They are members of the same club.
   d. Misaki is a friend from Rin's hometown.

2. Where did Rin go with Misaki?
   a. A bank
   b. A hospital
   c. A city hall
   d. A library

3. What ingredients need to become tender for the dish to be ready to serve?
   a. Pork
   b. Onion
   c. Carrots
   d. Water

Writing

A *Put the words in the correct order to complete the following sentences.*

1. (pickle / carrot and cabbage / Fee is / making).

_____

2. (the pickle / goes / well / with sandwiches / really)!

_____

B *Fill in the blanks with your opinion and then write a short essay.*

Step 1 Which do you prefer, cooking at home or eating out?

I prefer _____.

Step 2 What kind of meals do you like to eat?

I enjoy _____.

Step 3 Write down your opinion about the advantages of cooking at home or eating out.

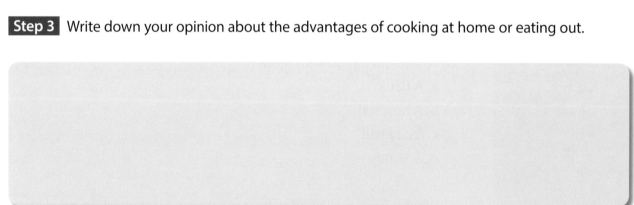

Language Box

Step 1. prefer A to B   prefer A rather than B   prefer to do A rather than to do B

....

Step 2. family   friend   communication   save money   healthy   difficult to cook at home
environment

UNIT 2 Boat Schools

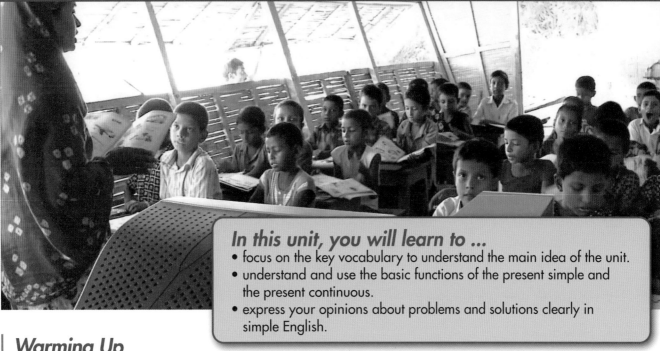

In this unit, you will learn to ...
- focus on the key vocabulary to understand the main idea of the unit.
- understand and use the basic functions of the present simple and the present continuous.
- express your opinions about problems and solutions clearly in simple English.

Warming Up

Choose your own answers to the following questions. Then ask your partner the questions.

1. What kind of school location would you like to study in?
   - ❏ A school in the forest
   - ❏ A school by the river
   - ❏ An urban school
   - ❏ Other (   )

2. How do you go to school?
   - ❏ On foot
   - ❏ By train
   - ❏ By bike
   - ❏ Other (   )

3. What do you know about Bangladesh?
   - ❏ History
   - ❏ Culture
   - ❏ Places
   - ❏ Other (   )

Watching

WEB動画 🖥 📀 DVD 💿 CD 07

Watch the video and write down some words or phrases that you hear. Then share them with your friends.

> Bangladesh

Vocabulary 🎧 08

A *Match the words and phrases below with the correct explanations (a – f).*

1. come together   ————   **a.** to make a group

2. climate   ————   **b.** to arrive at a place

3. architect   ————   **c.** a person who designs buildings

4. get to   ————   **d.** weather conditions

5. pick up   ————   **e.** to be a part of something

6. belong   ————   **f.** to give someone a ride in a vehicle

B *Fill in the blanks with words or phrases from Task A. Change the word form if necessary.*

1. I (   ) to a swimming club.

2. My uncle, who is a famous (   ), built my house.

3. How do we (   ) the nearest station?

Listening Comprehension WEB動画 📀DVD 🎧CD 07

A *Watch the video again and write T if the statement is true or F if it is false.*

1. Students travel by bus to get to their school.   ————

2. There are books in the boat school's classroom.   ————

3. Some students in the classroom can read English words aloud.   ————

4. All the students want to be architects.   ————

B *Arrange the main ideas in the order that they are mentioned in the video.*

Bangladesh now has more than 20 boat schools, and young and old students can study there.

These days, the climate is changing, and the rivers are growing in Bangladesh.

The classroom isn't big, but there are many tools to help students study.

_____ _____ _____

Tips on Listening and Speaking   🎧 09

Elision (1)
On some occasions, English speakers leave out a sound.
1. It's a hot day today, isn't it?
2. Please put that on the white table.

Dictation   🎧 10

Listen to the sentences and fill in the blanks.

1. It isn't easy for the children to (　　　　) (　　　　) school.

2. Water is a very big (　　　) of (　　　　) in Bangladesh.

3. They have boat (　　　　) too.

17

Retelling

WEB動画 🖥️ 🎞️ DVD

Watch part of the video again and tell the story of the scene to your partner. You can use the keywords below.

A lot of students _____.

Keywords study, boat school

In the boat school, _____.

Keywords desk, chair, book

A teacher and the students are _____.

Keywords read, book

Discussion

Fill in the blanks and exchange your ideas in pairs or small groups.

Step 1 A boat school improves their learning environment. What other problems do you think their learning environment still has?

It is difficult for them _____.

Step 2 What do you think is one of the solutions to this problem?

To solve this problem, we can _____.

Step 3 Discuss in group or pairs and evaluate each other's opinions. Based on your opinion, talk about which solutions you think are the most effective and why.

Language Box

Step 1. to buy stationery   to go to cram schools   to eat a nutritious lunch
to study Physical Education   to continue studying

Step 2. send stationery/money   build schools   improve public transportation
create job opportunities   train teachers

Step 3. excellent/good/fair/not good   too small/big   useful/useless fair/unfair
cost too much   children will not receive

Grammar

Present Simple and Present Continuous

Present Simple
① Regular habits
② General truth
③ Permanent situation

PAST ——— **THEN** ——— **NOW** ———▶ FUTURE

④ **Present Continuous**

①	I ride my bike to school.
②	The earth is round.
③	I have two sisters.
④	It is still raining outside.

Grammar Exercise

A *Choose the correct answer to complete the following sentences.*

1. The old woman usually (washes / is washing) clothes by the river.

2. It (snows / is snowing) outside now.

3. My brother (talks / is talking) on another phone now.

B *Put the words in the correct order to complete the following sentences.*

1. (we / the schedule / planning / are currently).

   _____

2. (the sun / around / goes / the earth).

   _____

3. (singing / loudly / who / is)?

   _____

🎧 11

As in many places around the world, there are many people in Bangladesh who live near bodies of water such as rivers or lakes. Their living environment provides plenty of opportunities for them to make a living from fishing, farming, and tourism. However, they also face a lot of difficulties.

5 First, they can't get enough education. Because of this, it is hard to find well-paying jobs, and so many of them live in poverty. Second, for water-based communities, industrialization has made life difficult. For example, waste from factories pollutes the water and brings health risks to the people living in such communities. Finally, the development of waterway transportation such as sightseeing boats breaks up water-based
10 homes and farms. It means people lose their homes and other resources that are necessary for life.

Living on the water involves a lot of difficulties. However, for the local people, it is their traditional way of life. Therefore, it is important to think of ways to support them while preserving their culture.

20

Vocabulary Check

Fill in the blanks with words from the word box below.

1. I use public (   ) every day.

2. I had (   ) solving the problem.

3. Many children in developing countries live in (   ).

> difficulty   poverty   transportation

Reading Comprehension

Read the article and choose the appropriate answer to the following questions.

1. Which of the following is a good point about living on the water?
   a. Health
   b. Tourism
   c. Architecture
   d. Education

2. What did industrialization bring?
   a. Pollution
   b. Unemployment
   c. Convenience
   d. Urbanization

3. What is important to consider when helping people living on the water?
   a. More houses
   b. Airports and airplanes
   c. Preserving traditional culture
   d. Industrialization

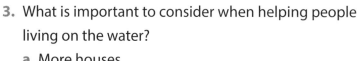

Writing

A *Put the words in the correct order to complete the following sentences.*

1. (the boat school / children / their homes / stops / near / to pick up).

   _____

2. (them / to / belongs / the future).

   _____

B *Fill in the blanks with your opinion and then write a short essay.*

Step 1 What do you think is the most serious problem for people who live on the water?

_____ is one of the most serious problems.

Step 2 What can we do to support the livelihoods of people living on the water?

We can _____ to support their livelihoods.

Step 3 Write your opinion about problems and solutions for people living on the water.

Language Box

Step 1. global warming   pollution   education   health problems   job opportunities

Step 2. save electricity   reduce waste   stop industrializing   work together   build hospitals

Colors in the UK

In this unit, you will learn to ...
- focus on the key vocabulary to understand the main idea of the unit.
- understand and use the basic functions of *will* and *be going to*.
- describe what you see and express your opinions clearly in simple English.

Warming Up

Choose your own answers to the following questions. Then ask your partner the questions.

1. What is famous in your hometown?
   - ❏ Food
   - ❏ Old buildings
   - ❏ Nature
   - ❏ Other ( )

2. Where do you want to live in the future?
   - ❏ A big city
   - ❏ An island
   - ❏ The countryside
   - ❏ Other ( )

3. What do you know about the UK?
   - ❏ History
   - ❏ Culture
   - ❏ Place
   - ❏ Other ( )

Watching   WEB動画 🖥 📀 DVD 💿 CD 12

Watch the video and write down some words or phrases that you hear. Then share them with your friends.

UK (United Kingdom)

Vocabulary 🎧 13

A *Match the words below with the correct explanations (a – f).*

1. capital   _____   **a.** the direction that is usually at the top of a map

2. modern   _____   **b.** new and up to date

3. busy   _____   **c.** the most important city of a country

4. double-decker   _____   **d.** a very tall building

5. skyscraper   _____   **e.** a bus with two floors

6. north   _____   **f.** full of people or vehicles

B *Fill in the blanks with words from Task A. Change the word form if necessary.*

1. I read some (   ) literature about the countryside.

2. It is hard to walk on a (   ) road.

3. Tokyo is the (   ) of Japan.

Listening Comprehension   WEB動画 🖥 📀 DVD 🎧 CD 12

A *Watch the video again and write T if the statement is true or F if it is false.*

1. All the buildings in London are tall and old.   _____

2. There are some pretty houses in London.   _____

3. The Lake District is close to London.   _____

4. We can see natural beauty in the Lake District.   _____

B *Check the colors that are mentioned in the video.*

⬤	⬤	⬤	⬤	⬤
☐	☐	☐	☐	☐
red	**green**	**black**	**light blue**	**dark blue**

☐	☐	☐	☐	☐
purple	sky blue	light pink	gray	brown

Tips on Listening and Speaking 🎧 14

Linking (1)

The final sound of a word sometimes connects with the first sound of the next.

1. I need your help.
2. Have you ever been abroad?
3. Do it right now!

Dictation 🎧 15

Listen to the sentences and fill in the blanks.

1. (   ) (   ) rains, however, the lakes look gray.

2. The streets are busy during the (   ) (   ) (   ).

3. Five hundred kilometers north of London is the Lake District. It's (   )
(   ) its lakes and mountains.

cloudy and rainy

Lake District

25

Retelling

Watch part of the video again and tell the story of the scene to your partner. You can use the keywords below.

The Lake District is _____.
Keywords famous for, lake, mountain

We can see _____.
Keywords beautiful, nature

There are _____.
Keywords colorful, mountain

Discussion

Fill in the blanks and exchange your ideas in pairs or small groups.

Step 1 What do you think is a good point of living in a city?

I think _____.

Step 2 What do you think is a good point of living in the countryside?

I think _____.

Step 3 Discuss in groups or pairs and evaluate each other's opinions. Based on your opinion, talk about which place is better for you to live in and why.

Language Box

Step 1. convenience   enjoyable places   big shopping malls

....

Step 2. beautiful nature   fresh crops   clean air

Grammar

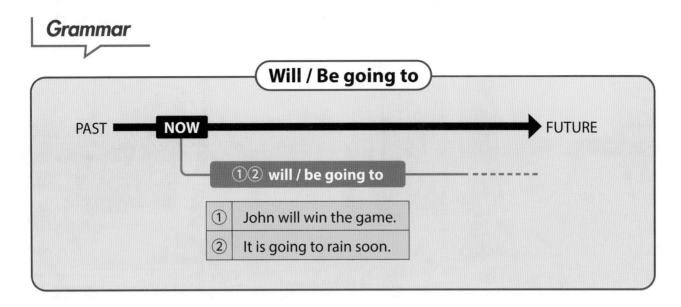

Grammar Exercise

A *Rewrite the following sentences using the words in brackets.*

1. The baby walks. [will]

_____

2. My son works in a company. [be going to]

_____

3. The students do their homework in the classroom. [will]

_____

B *Put the words in the correct order to complete the following sentences.*

1. (play / we / soccer / with / will / my friends).

_____

2. (will / the train / at / arrive / the station).

_____

3. (Mary / going / go / shopping / is / to).

_____

UNIT 1 UNIT 2 UNIT 3 UNIT 4 UNIT 5 UNIT 6 UNIT 7 UNIT 8 UNIT 9 UNIT 10 UNIT 11 UNIT 12 UNIT 13 UNIT 14 UNIT 15

Profile
Name: Susan
Age: 19 years old   (a university student)

I moved to Tokyo as an exchange student just three days ago to enjoy university life. Today, I walked around my new home. This was the first time for me to
5 *go out in Tokyo!*

I found Tokyo was totally different from my hometown. There were a lot of skyscrapers, apartments, and shopping malls in Tokyo. Main streets were always crowded, and people walked at a quick pace. To tell the truth, I got lost in the closest station today. I was used to the unmanned station in my hometown. Compared with that, the station near my new home
10 *seemed very big to me. Surprisingly, there are at least 5 exits in that station! Inside the station, it was hard for me to find the right exit. I was confused about which direction I should go. I've never been so glad to have a smartphone with a map app in my life.*

Everything I saw today was fresh and I felt excited. Although I am a bit nervous about my new life in Tokyo, I will do my best. After I get used to the life here, I want to invite my parents.

Vocabulary Check

Fill in the blanks with words from the word box below.

1. In the morning, I have to take the most (   ) train.

2. When we stay at a hotel, we should check where the emergency (   ) is.

3. Nick was (   ) to hear the news.

exit   crowded   confused

Reading Comprehension

Read the article and choose the appropriate answer to the following questions.

1. Which statement is true about Susan's hometown?
   a. It has big buildings.
   b. There are a lot of university students.
   c. It has a station with no staff.
   d. It has a traditional shopping mall.

2. Why did Susan come to Tokyo?
   a. To go shopping with her family
   b. To watch a soccer game
   c. To study in a famous library
   d. To go to university

3. How did she overcome her difficulty in the station in Tokyo?
   a. She bought a new smartphone.
   b. She used an app to check the directions.
   c. She asked people which exit to take.
   d. She walked quickly.

UNIT 1 UNIT 2 UNIT 3 UNIT 4 UNIT 5 UNIT 6 UNIT 7 UNIT 8 UNIT 9 UNIT 10 UNIT 11 UNIT 12 UNIT 13 UNIT 14 UNIT 15

Writing

A *Put the words in the correct order to complete the following sentences.*

1. (black taxis / London / is / its / for / famous).

   _____

2. (for / around the lakes / many people / long walks / go).

   _____

B *Fill in the blanks with your opinion and then write a short essay.*

Step 1 What is a good point of your hometown?

   One good point of my hometown is _____.

Step 2 If you could make a tour plan for your hometown, where would you recommend?

   I would recommend _____.

Step 3 Introduce your hometown.

Language Box

Step 1. nature   delicious crops   convenience   many places to enjoy

Step 2. famous amusement park   old temple   famous restaurant   beautiful mountain
        big shopping mall

Homes on Wheels

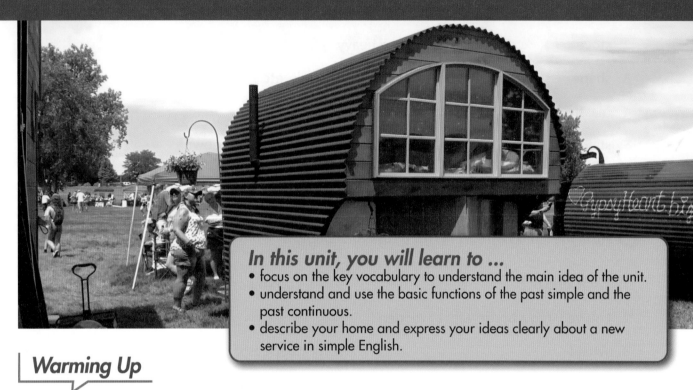

GypsyHeart.biz

In this unit, you will learn to ...
- focus on the key vocabulary to understand the main idea of the unit.
- understand and use the basic functions of the past simple and the past continuous.
- describe your home and express your ideas clearly about a new service in simple English.

Warming Up

Choose your own answers to the following questions. Then ask your partner the questions.

1. Have you ever moved?
   - ❑ No   ❑ Once
   - ❑ Twice   ❑ _____ times

2. Do you have any of the following in your home?
   - ❑ A kitchen   ❑ Stairs
   - ❑ A loft   ❑ Plants

3. When do you think is the best time to buy a house?
   - ❑ After starting a job   ❑ After getting married
   - ❑ After you have had a child   ❑ Other (   )

Watching
WEB動画 🖥️ 📀 DVD 💿 CD 17

Watch the video and write down some words or phrases that you hear. Then share them with your friends.

wheels

Vocabulary

🎧 18

A *Match the words below with the correct explanations (a – f).*

1. tiny _____
2. stove _____
3. shape _____
4. massive _____
5. staircase _____
6. mobile _____

a. to be able to move or be moved easily
b. big and heavy
c. circle, square, triangle, etc.
d. very small
e. a set of steps used to go up and down
f. a device that provides heat for cooking

B *Fill in the blanks with words from Task A. Change the word form if necessary.*

1. What kind of (   ) do you prefer, gas or electric?

2. I moved into a house with a wooden (   ).

3. What (   ) is your pen case?

Listening Comprehension

WEB動画 📀 DVD 🎧 CD 17

A *Watch the video again and write T if the statement is true or F if it is false.*

1. The homes have wheels so they can move to different places. _____

2. One of the homes is made of beautiful wood. _____

3. None of the homes has a bedroom with a big bed. _____

4. Bee and Theo don't have lots of ideas for their own home on wheels. _____

B *Check the things that homes in the video have.*

☐ kitchen   ☐ big bed   ☐ wheel   ☐ window

32

 □ air conditioner

 □ staircase

 □ TV

 □ guitar

 □ bike

 □ showerhead

Tips on Listening and Speaking 🎧 19

Contractions (2)
Some verbs such as "be" and "have" have a short form in speech.

1. You gave us a lot of books, but <u>we've</u> lost them all.
2. <u>He's</u> dressed in a red suit that he bought yesterday.
3. <u>I've</u> been working on the road.

Dictation 🎧 20

Listen to the sentences and fill in the blanks.

1. (   ) all got wheels.

2. (   ) going on, guys?

3. (   ) a bookcase for your books (   ) all your things.

bookcase

Retelling 📺 💿

Watch part of the video again and tell the story of the scene to your partner. You can use the keywords below.

A couple is _____ .
Keywords look, inside, home

The kitchen has _____ .
Keywords stove, sink, shelf

We can _____ .
Keywords cook, food, wash

Discussion

Fill in the blanks and exchange your ideas in pairs or small groups.

Step 1 How many rooms do you have in your house?

I have _____ rooms in my house, including _____ ,

_____ , and _____ .

Step 2 What do you have in your house?

I have _____ , _____ and _____ in

my house.

Step 3 Ask your partner to describe their home. Find some similarities and differences between your answers. A fictional story is fine.

Language Box

Step 1. kitchen   living room   bedroom   restroom   training room   bathroom
theater room

....

Step 2. desk   drawer   closet   electric kettle   stairs   washstand   bookshelf   bed

....

Step 3. I have the same thing.   I don't have any …   I want to buy …   I used to have one.

Grammar

Past Simple and Past Continuous

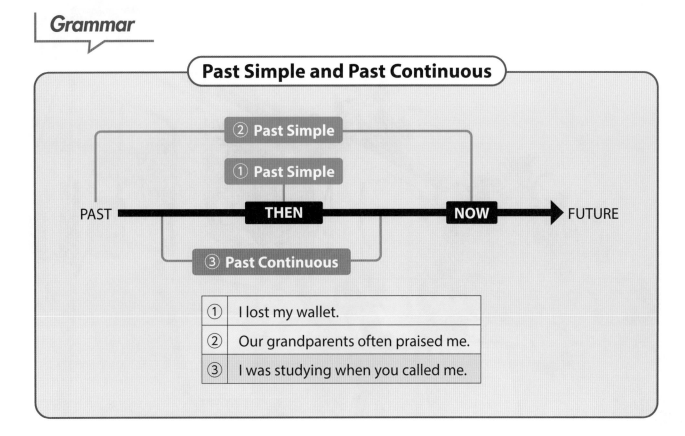

①	I lost my wallet.
②	Our grandparents often praised me.
③	I was studying when you called me.

Grammar Exercise

A *Choose the correct answer to complete the following sentences.*

1. Rie (was lying / lay) on the bed when I called her.

2. My sister (left / leaves) my house last year.

3. I (was playing / played) the trumpet when you came into the room.

B *Put the words in the correct order to complete the following sentences.*

1. (the dog / at / barking / that time / was).

   _____

2. (the news / I / surprised / hear / was / to).

   _____

3. (bought / and / Ken / gave it / to his girlfriend / a ring).

   _____

🎧 21

Camper vans, which are a combination of homes and wheels, enable us to camp anywhere. Similar to this, mobile services are changing our lifestyles. Some traditional services were often tied to a specific place. For example, we had to go to a library to borrow a book. Here are some examples of mobile services.

Mobile retail vehicles

5

These are like mini-convenience stores on wheels. They sell fresh food and other goods to people living in rural areas or those who have difficulty going to a store. Even major convenience store chains in Japan are doing this.

Food trucks

10

We can find kitchens on wheels mainly in cities and buy some freshly cooked dishes. For owners, this is great because they can start with a small amount of money. For customers, the trucks allow them to enjoy food in their own home or office.

Furthermore, there are other cool mobile services! We already have mobile libraries, blood donation buses, mobile fashion trucks, and even ambulances with operating rooms.

15 These services have wheels, so they can go where they're needed. Although they face challenges like bad weather or limited stock, they have the potential to change our customs.

Vocabulary Check

Fill in the blanks with words from the word box below.

1. Red and white is a good (   ).

2. (   ) need to be informed of prices in advance.

3. There's one more injured person here, so please call another
(   ).

combination	customers	ambulance

Reading Comprehension

Read the article and choose the appropriate answer to the following questions.

1. What are mobile retail vehicles like?
   a. A supermarket
   b. A convenience store
   c. A hospital
   d. A library

2. What is an advantage of kitchen trucks for owners?
   a. Less expensive to start
   b. Enjoyable to work in
   c. Connected to customers
   d. Easy to make money

3. Which other mobile service is mentioned in the article?
   a. Mobile fashion trucks
   b. Mobile dentists
   c. Mobile barbers
   d. Mobile spas

UNIT 1 UNIT 2 UNIT 3 UNIT 4 UNIT 5 UNIT 6 UNIT 7 UNIT 8 UNIT 9 UNIT 10 UNIT 11 UNIT 12 UNIT 13 UNIT 14 UNIT 15

Writing

A *Put the words in the correct order to complete the following sentences.*

1. (in many different / lots of / homes here / shapes and sizes / there / are).

   _____

2. (all the same / are / in / these homes / one way).

   _____

B *Fill in the blanks with your opinion and then write a short essay.*

Step 1 Create your own mobile service.

   I want to create _____.

Step 2 Who would benefit from your mobile service?

   _____ would benefit from it.

Step 3 Try to think of a new kind of mobile service and write your thoughts about it.

Language Box

Step 1. barber   hospital   bank   post office   city hall   spa   flower shop   library

Step 2. elderly people   students   business persons   people living in remote areas
people living in urban areas   young adults

38

Maddy in the City

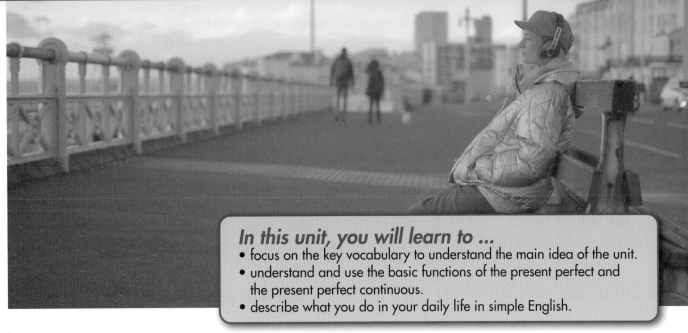

In this unit, you will learn to ...
• focus on the key vocabulary to understand the main idea of the unit.
• understand and use the basic functions of the present perfect and the present perfect continuous.
• describe what you do in your daily life in simple English.

Warming Up

Choose your own answers to the following questions. Then ask your partner the questions.

1. What kind of videos do you watch on the Internet?
   ❑ Games   ❑ Food
   ❑ Vlogs   ❑ Other (   )

2. How do you use social media?
   ❑ Send text messages   ❑ Share images/videos
   ❑ Just read posts   ❑ Other (   )

3. What is the most important thing in your daily life?
   ❑ Food   ❑ Sleep
   ❑ Study   ❑ Other (   )

Watching WEB動画 🖥 DVD 🔊 CD 22

Watch the video and write down some words or phrases that you hear. Then share them with your friends.

living

Vocabulary 🎧 23

(A) *Match the words below with the correct explanations (a – f).*

1. routine   _____   **a.** happening or done every day

2. production   _____   **b.** a system of exercises for relaxation

3. performer   _____   **c.** the act or process of making a music or video product

4. yoga   _____   **d.** the process of making or growing things to be sold

5. daily   _____   **e.** the usual order in which you do things

6. recording   _____   **f.** a person who sings or acts for an audience

(B) *Fill in the blanks with words from Task A. Change the word form if necessary.*

1. Exercise is part of my (   ) every morning.

2. (   ) movies is prohibited in the cinema.

3. My uncle was a street (   ) 15 years ago.

Listening Comprehension WEB動画 📀 DVD 🎧 CD 22

(A) *Watch the video again and write T if the statement is true or F if it is false.*

1. Maddy works as a server in a café.   _____

2. Maddy spends all day singing.   _____

3. Maddy goes to the recording studio in the afternoon.   _____

4. Maddy doesn't eat dinner.   _____

(B) *Arrange the activities in the order that Maddy does them.*

goes to the café

has breakfast

goes to the studio

cooks dinner

goes shopping

has lunch

does yoga

_____ ➡ _____ ➡ _____

➡ _____ ➡ _____ ➡ _____

➡ _____

Tips on Listening and Speaking 🔊 24

Assimilation (1)
Some speech sounds change and become more similar to the sound just before or after them.

1. That theater is the biggest in our town.
2. Could you come with me?
3. Of course, food is a very important part of that celebration as well.

Dictation 🔊 25

Listen to the sentences and fill in the blanks.

1. Maddy (   ) (   ).

2. In the studio, (   ) (   )!

3. She has (   ) (   ) day tomorrow.

Retelling ⬜📱 💿

Watch part of the video again and tell the story of the scene to your partner. You can use the keywords below.

Maddy _____ .
Keywords go, shopping, buy

Maddy _____ .
Keywords cook, dinner

Staying healthy _____ .
Keywords important, when, busy

Discussion

Fill in the blanks and exchange your ideas in pairs or small groups.

Step 1 What is the first thing you do when you wake up in the morning?

I _____ first every morning.

Step 2 What do you usually do before going to bed?

I usually _____ every night before going to bed.

Step 3 Ask your partner about his or her daily routine and compare it with yours. How is it similar and different?

Language Box

Step 1. go to the bathroom   brush teeth   eat breakfast   drink water   watch TV   go jogging

Step 2. browse the internet   play games   read books   do homework   take a shower

Step 3. first   second   third   then   next   after that   following that   finally

Grammar

Present Perfect and Present Perfect Continuous

①② **Present Perfect**

PAST ━━ **THEN** ━━━━━━━━━━━━━━ **NOW** ━━▶ FUTURE

③ **Present Perfect Continuous**

①	Sam's baby has been ill since last week.
②	I have bought a house in Tokyo.
③	Meg has been singing every morning since last year.

Grammar Exercise

A *Choose the correct answer to complete the following sentences.*

1. Our parents (have loved / have been loving) that food since a while ago.

2. John (has talked / has been talking) on the phone to a customer for more than an hour so far.

3. It (has been raining / has rained) non-stop since early this morning.

B *Put the words in the correct order to complete the following sentences.*

1. (the company / since / doing a survey / preferences / its customers' / has / understood).

   _____

2. (have / many viewers / since its release / on that video / posting their comments / been).

   _____

3. (I / following / since I got married / have / a daily routine / been).

   _____

UNIT 1 UNIT 2 UNIT 3 UNIT 4 UNIT 5 UNIT 6 UNIT 7 UNIT 8 UNIT 9 UNIT 10 UNIT 11 UNIT 12 UNIT 13 UNIT 14 UNIT 15

Comments from viewers on Maddy's video

Lisa:

This video was really interesting. I was impressed by Maddy's ability to lead a busy life learning music while maintaining a healthy lifestyle. I'm inspired to follow her example and have a healthy diet even when I'm busy.

Judy:

It was very helpful to find out about the life of a music student. I'm a high
5 school student, and I'm considering studying music in college. I heard that Maddy is studying music production. Maddy, when did you start studying music production? Is there anything I should do while in high school?

Nick:

It's great that you're doing exercise. To create good music, we need physical strength, and lung capacity, but many people neglect basic training like yoga.
10 I hope everyone can learn from your videos.

Vocabulary Check

Fill in the blanks with words from the word box below.

1. It is important to (   ) good relations with viewers.

2. You must also (   ) things from a legal point of view.

3. Which is more important, (   ) health or mental health?

> maintain   physical   consider

Reading Comprehension

Read the article and choose the appropriate answer to the following questions.

1. Who is a high school student?
   a. Lisa
   b. Judy
   c. Nick
   d. Maddy

2. What does Lisa want to do after watching Maddy's story?
   a. Have a healthy diet
   b. Create songs
   c. Do exercise
   d. Study at a café

3. What does Nick think is important in creating songs?
   a. Physical strength
   b. Sense of rhythm
   c. Sense of humor
   d. Knowledge

Writing

A *Put the words in the correct order to complete the following sentences.*

1. (Maddy / and does / morning yoga / brushes / her / her teeth).

   _____

2. (is / exercise / very / a musician and performer / for / important).

   _____

B *Fill in the blanks with your opinion and then write a paragraph.*

Step 1 Which activity did you like the most in Maddy's video?

   I liked _____.

Step 2 What do you think about that activity?

   I _____.

Step 3 Write your own comment on the video that you could post on social media.

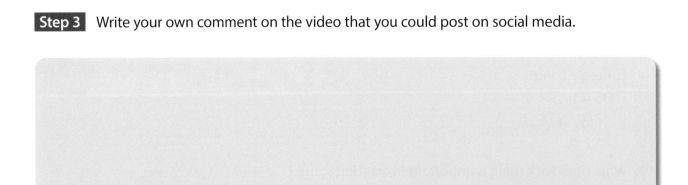

Language Box

Step 1. go to the café   have breakfast   make music   cook dinner   go shopping
have lunch   do yoga

Step 2. be moved   want to do the same thing   be doing the same thing   difficult to do that
let my friends know

Falcons at Work

In this unit, you will learn to ...
- focus on the key vocabulary to understand the main idea of the unit.
- understand and use the basic functions of the past simple and the present perfect.
- express your opinions clearly about friendship (including that with pets) in simple English.

Warming Up

Choose your own answers to the following questions. Then ask your partner the questions.

1. Do you have any pets?
   - ❏ Dog
   - ❏ Cat
   - ❏ Fish
   - ❏ Other ( )

2. If you could keep any animal, what would you like to have?
   - ❏ Horse
   - ❏ Falcon
   - ❏ Snake
   - ❏ Other ( )

3. What do you think is difficult about having pets?
   - ❏ Health care
   - ❏ Cost
   - ❏ Space
   - ❏ Other ( )

Watching   WEB動画 🖥 📀 DVD 📀 CD 27

Watch the video and write down some words or phrases that you hear. Then share them with your friends.

> *two children*

Vocabulary 🎧 28

A *Match the words and phrases below with the correct explanations (a – f).*

1. own　　　———　　　**a.** a person who hunts with birds

2. train　　　———　　　**b.** to have something oneself

3. fly away　　———　　**c.** a person who is taught how to do a job

4. part of　　———　　　**d.** some but not all

5. trainee　　———　　　**e.** to teach skills

6. falconer　　———　　　**f.** to escape using wings

B *Fill in the blanks with words or phrases from Task A. Change the word form if necessary.*

1. They (　　　　　　　　　　　) dogs using balls.

2. I am just a small (　　　　　　　　　　　) modern society.

3. We (　　　　　　　　) two new cars.

Listening Comprehension 💻WEB動画 📀DVD 🎧 27

A *Watch the video again and write T if the statement is true or F if it is false.*

1. Steve owns several kinds of birds.　　　　　　　　　　　———

2. Steve and Harriet have been good friends for a long time.　———

3. Steve and Harriet work even at night.　　　　　　　　　　———

4. Steve treats his birds as family.　　　　　　　　　　　　———

B *Arrange the main ideas in the order that they are mentioned in the video.*

A falconer owns birds and trains them as pets.

48

Harriet learns how to call a hawk.

Birds are a very different kind of pet. But Steve and his birds are great friends.

 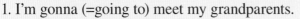

Tips on Listening and Speaking   🎧 29

Assimilation (2)
In some cases, two words combine a different word.

1. I'm gonna (=going to) meet my grandparents.
2. What do you wanna (=want to) eat for lunch?
3. We've gotta (=got to) go.

Dictation   🎧 30

Listen to the sentences and fill in the blanks.

1. Today, we're (   ) (   ) here, training up Harriet and our new rescued Harris hawk, Archie.

2. I've (   ) do it right now.

3. Dogs are man's best friends. But (   ) (   ) birds?

Retelling

WEB動画 🖥 💿DVD

Watch part of the video again and tell the story of the scene to your partner. You can use the keywords below.

A falconer is a person who _____.
Keywords own, train, pets

A falconer and a falcon _____.
Keywords make, friend

By training, falconers learn _____.
Keywords how, call

Discussion

Fill in the blanks and exchange your ideas in pairs or small groups.

Step 1 Besides dogs, what animals do you think could be considered man's best friends?

I think _____ could be man's best friends.

Step 2 Why did you choose that animal?

I chose it because _____.

Step 3 Share your opinion in groups or pairs.

Language Box

Step 1. monkeys   cats   birds   horses   chimpanzees

....

Step 2. are smart   are kind   understand our feelings   remember our face

Grammar

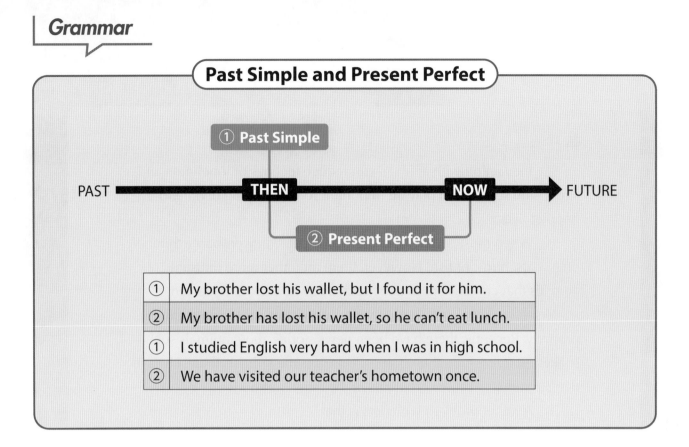

Past Simple and Present Perfect

①	My brother lost his wallet, but I found it for him.
②	My brother has lost his wallet, so he can't eat lunch.
①	I studied English very hard when I was in high school.
②	We have visited our teacher's hometown once.

Grammar Exercise

A *Choose the correct answer to complete the following sentences.*

1. I (talked / have talked) to you three days ago.

2. The driver (went / has gone) to the supermarket yesterday.

3. We (knew / have known) each other since we were children.

B *Put the words in the correct order to complete the following sentences.*

1. (joined / team / the / he / baseball).

   _____

2. (Australia / to / been / my sister / has).

   _____

3. (before / I / seen / have / him).

   _____

🎵 31

Interaction with animals can reduce feelings of loneliness and stress, and so pets can play an important role in helping people to live happier lives.

When most people hear the word "pet," they probably think of
5 dogs, cats, birds, or fish. However, there are other more unusual animals that can be kept as pets, such as owls, snakes, and even spiders. If we keep a pet, we must be responsible for looking after it properly. Recently, there have been news stories about animals such as snakes escaping from their homes. This puts the animals themselves in
10 danger and also causes problems in the neighborhood.

Another problem with pets is that some owners get tired of them and sometimes throw them out. In order to solve this problem, some cities and towns
15 have set up animal shelters. Even though the number of "shelter animals" has decreased over the past few years, there are still many animals that have no home to return to because of problems with their
20 owners. In some cases, shelter animals have to be killed because they are too expensive to keep. If you would like to help with this serious problem, why not visit a shelter in your neighborhood? This
25 will allow you to meet shelter animals and adopt one if you think you can take on the responsibility.

Vocabulary Check

Fill in the blanks with words from the word box below.

1. I want to talk about your (   ) in the project.

2. Your bag is more (   ) than mine.

3. The typhoon (   ) a lot of damage to buildings in the town.

> expensive   role   caused

Reading Comprehension

Read the article and choose the appropriate answer to the following questions.

1. What feeling may people have when they interact with their pets?
   a. Loneliness
   b. Fear
   c. Excitement
   d. Happiness

2. What problem is mentioned in the passage?
   a. Unwanted animals
   b. Decreasing demand for pets
   c. Dangerous big pets
   d. A lack of animal shelters

3. Who do you think would be a suitable owner for a shelter animal?
   a. Someone who is rich
   b. Someone who is responsible
   c. Someone who has medical knowledge
   d. Someone who loves the outdoors

Writing

A *Put the words in the correct order to complete the following sentences.*

1. (my family / birds / my / of / part / are).

   _____

2. (going / Harriet / we are / to / training up / be here).

   _____

B *Fill in the blanks with your opinion and then write a short essay.*

Step 1 There are a lot of shelter dogs and cats in Japan. Why does this happen? Answer with your own ideas.

It happens because _____.

Step 2 What do you think is the best solution to this problem?

To solve this problem, I think _____.

Step 3 Write your opinion about having pets.

Language Box

Step 1. cost a lot of money   too busy to have pets   lack of affection   lose interest

Step 2. give owners a subsidy   make shots free   explain more about the reality of having pets
show the reality of shelter pets

54

Diwali in New York

In this unit, you will learn to ...
- focus on the key vocabulary to understand the main idea of the unit.
- understand and use the basic functions of the past perfect and the past simple.
- describe events or festivals you are familiar with in simple English.

Warming Up

Choose your own answers to the following questions. Then ask your partner the questions.

1. What kind of festivals do you have in your area?
   - ❑ Summer festival
   - ❑ Snow festival
   - ❑ Autumn festival
   - ❑ Other ( )

2. Have you ever attended a festival?
   - ❑ Yes, every year.
   - ❑ Yes, but rarely.
   - ❑ Yes, sometimes.
   - ❑ No, I haven't

3. Which do you think is the most important cultural tradition to preserve?
   - ❑ Clothing
   - ❑ Festivals
   - ❑ Food and drink
   - ❑ Other ( )

Watching

WEB動画 🖥️ 📀 DVD 📀 CD 32

Watch the video and write down some words or phrases that you hear. Then share them with your friends.

New York

Vocabulary

🔊 33

A *Match the words below with the correct explanations (a – f).*

1. goat _____   **a.** the power to make something work

2. plenty _____   **b.** the act of marking a special occasion

3. energy _____   **c.** an animal with horns on its head and long hair under its chin

4. whole _____   **d.** a public event connected with a particular religion or activity

5. celebration _____   **e.** a large quantity that is enough or more than enough

6. festival _____   **f.** all of something

B *Fill in the blanks with words from Task A. Change the word form if necessary.*

1. There is (   ) of food in the fridge.

2. I'll invite some friends to my family's New Year (   ).

3. Running fast takes a lot of (   ).

Listening Comprehension

WEB動画 🖥 📀 DVD 🔊 CD 32

A *Watch the video again and write T if the statement is true or F if it is false.*

1. Diwali is the Hindu festival of food. _____

2. Burfi is a traditional Indian sweet. _____

3. At the Diwali festival in New York, people try Indian food in the street. _____

4. Mickela loves Indian dancing. _____

B *Check which foods are mentioned in the video.*

☐ hamburger   ☐ tandoori chicken   ☐ potato   ☐ goat curry

☐ fries   ☐ rice   ☐ burfi   ☐ chickpeas

Tips on Listening and Speaking 🎧 34

Weakening (1)

Weakening happens especially at the end of function words such as prepositions, and pronouns, and some verbs.

1. What <u>would</u> happen in the classroom?
2. You <u>were</u> in the natural history museum, right?
3. My mother should get <u>to</u> the hall before noon.

Dictation 🎧 35

Listen to the sentences and fill in the blanks.

1. Share (   ) culture (   ) the whole city.

2. They are (   ) Diwali together!

3. And all that delicious Diwali food gives her plenty of (   ).

Retelling

WEB動画 🖥 💿 DVD

Watch part of the video again and tell the story of the scene to your partner. You can use the keywords below.

There is _____.
Keywords street, festival, New York

Mickela _____.
Keywords dance, performance, stage

It's _____.
Keywords chance, share, culture

Discussion

Fill in the blanks and exchange your ideas in pairs or small groups.

Step 1 What kind of traditional events do you have in your hometown?

In my hometown, there is/are _____.

Step 2 What do you do at the event(s)?

I _____ at the event.

Step 3 Ask your partner about traditional event(s) in their hometown and what they think of it, and share your own thoughts on it.

Language Box

Step 1. season   festival   snow   fire   shrine   temple   nature

....

Step 2. sing songs   dance   play musical instruments   eat traditional food
get to know the local area   get along with others

58

Grammar

Past Perfect and Past Simple

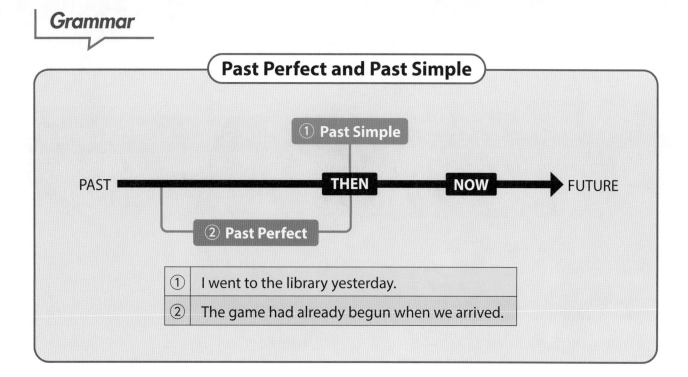

| ① | I went to the library yesterday. |
| ② | The game had already begun when we arrived. |

Grammar Exercise

A *Choose the correct answer to complete the following sentences.*

1. My relative was able to buy the apartment because he (had saved / has saved) money for 15 years before buying it.

2. Yuta said he (had been / went) to several districts before he went to the oldest district.

3. Construction at the station (started / had started) at 10 o'clock yesterday.

B *Put the words in the correct order to complete the following sentences.*

1. (it / to have / exciting / was / books / new).

   _____

2. (100 items / had / the shop / we / before closing / sold).

   _____

3. (before / had / the zoo opened / for two hours / a family / waited in line).

   _____

UNIT 1 UNIT 2 UNIT 3 UNIT 4 UNIT 5 UNIT 6 **UNIT 7** UNIT 8 UNIT 9 UNIT 10 UNIT 11 UNIT 12 UNIT 13 UNIT 14 UNIT 15

🎵 36

New Year's Day in Japan is generally celebrated on January 1st with special meals and customs. However, celebrations are different in other countries.

Diwali is a festival for celebrating the Hindu New Year. In India, the new year starts in late October or early November. It is celebrated as a public holiday.
5 Hinduism is one of the world's largest religions and is more than twice as large as Buddhism. Therefore, a lot of people around the world celebrate Diwali.

In Japan, people in some regions celebrate New Year's Day in late January or early February based on the traditional Japanese calendar. This is called the "Lunar New Year." It is also celebrated in many other Asian countries, including
10 China. Chinese people call it the "Spring Festival."

In some countries, Christmas celebrations are more important than New Year's Day. So, why not consider participating in some events that celebrate the New Year in different ways from your own custom?

Vocabulary Check

Fill in the blanks with words from the word box below.

1. Several large (　　　　) began in the same place.

2. The meaning of a word might change depending on the (　　　　) of the country.

3. Our ancestors created the (　　　　) of celebrating a new year.

| custom | region | religions |

Reading Comprehension

Read the article and choose the appropriate answer to the following questions.

1. How often is Diwali held?
   a. Once a year
   b. Twice a year
   c. Every month
   d. Every other month

2. In which month does the New Year begin in the traditional Japanese calendar?
   a. February
   b. March
   c. September
   d. December

3. Which is larger, Buddhism or Hinduism?
   a. Buddhism
   b. Hinduism
   c. They are the same size.
   d. This is not mentioned.

Writing

A *Put the words in the correct order to complete the following sentences.*

1. (there / left / before / isn't / much time / the dance performance).

   _____

2. (to perform / stage / our Bhangra song / about to / we're / go on)!

   _____

B *Fill in the blanks with your opinion and then write a short essay.*

Step 1   What events around you originated in a foreign country?

_____ came from abroad.

Step 2   What has been your experience with such events so far?

I _____ .

Step 3   Write your comments on events that originated in a foreign country.

Language Box

Step 1. Thanksgiving Day	Halloween	Christmas	*Tanabata*	St. Valentine's Day	*Obon*

Step 2. participate   sing   dance   buy   give   practice   wear   gifts   costume

Chloe the Upcycler

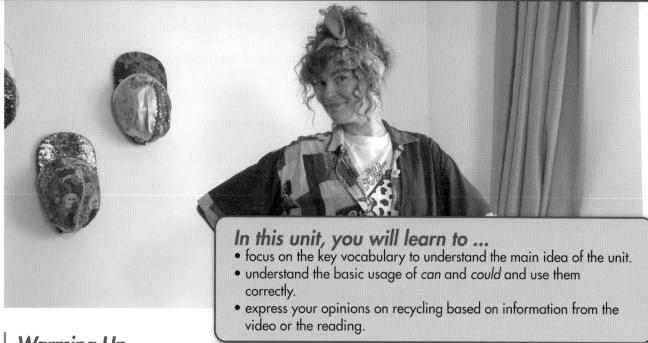

In this unit, you will learn to ...
- focus on the key vocabulary to understand the main idea of the unit.
- understand the basic usage of *can* and *could* and use them correctly.
- express your opinions on recycling based on information from the video or the reading.

Warming Up

Choose your own answers to the following questions. Then ask your partner the questions.

1. What do you do to prevent environmental problems?
   - ❑ Reduce waste
   - ❑ Recycle resources
   - ❑ Buy reused products
   - ❑ Other ( )

2. Which of these do you recycle?
   - ❑ Clothes
   - ❑ Plastic bottles
   - ❑ Paper
   - ❑ Other ( )

3. Which of the following do you think is the most serious problem?
   - ❑ Rising sea levels
   - ❑ Air pollution
   - ❑ Extinction of animals
   - ❑ Other ( )

Watching   WEB動画 🖥️ 📀DVD 📀CD 37

Watch the video and write down some words or phrases that you hear. Then share them with your friends.

shopping street

Vocabulary 🎧 38

A *Match the words below with the correct explanations (a – f).*

1. a pair of _____   **a.** picturing something in your mind

2. material _____   **b.** what things are made of

3. label _____   **c.** two things that are used together

4. neighborhood _____   **d.** a brand that makes products such as clothes or music

5. imagination _____   **e.** a precious thing or person

6. treasure _____   **f.** the area around where you live

B *Fill in the blanks with words or phrases from Task A.*

1. I want to buy (   ) glasses.

2. The beautiful ring that my mother gave me is my (   ).

3. What (   ) is this shirt made of?

Listening Comprehension 📺WEB動画 📀DVD 37

A *Watch the video again and write T if the statement is true or F if it is false.*

1. The main shopping street is the Cowley Road. _____

2. It is easy to find Chloe in the main shopping street. _____

3. Chloe makes many colorful clothes to give to her family. _____

4. Chloe wants to tell people that it is easy and fun to make things ourselves. _____

B *Arrange the main ideas in the order that they are mentioned in the video.*

Chloe uses old clothes and accessories to make new ones.

Think of something you can do with the materials.

Chloe does more than sell her own clothes.

_____  _____ _____

Tips on Listening and Speaking 🎧 39

Linking (2)

The final sound of a word sometimes connects with the first sound of the next. Sometimes phrases with more than three words sound like one word.

1. Take it easy.
2. Check it out.
3. I'll keep in touch with you.

Dictation 🎧 40

Listen to the sentences and fill in the blanks.

1. Is it (   ) (   ) as she says it is?

2. Have a (   ) (   ) you.

3. The real treasures often look like rubbish until you
   pick (   ) (   ).

65

Retelling

Watch part of the video again and tell the story of the scene to your partner. You can use the keywords below.

Chloe uses _____.
> **keywords** clothes, accessory, new product

It is fun to _____.
> **keywords** make, new product, clothes, accessory

When Chloe goes shopping, she _____.
> **keywords** look for, idea

Discussion

Fill in the blanks and exchange your ideas in pairs or small groups.

Step 1 What do you do with the clothes when you can no longer wear them?

I usually _____.

Step 2 What can you make with clothes you no longer wear?

I can make _____ from _____.

Step 3 Discuss in group or pairs and evaluate each other's opinions. Based on your opinion, talk about which solutions you think are the most attractive and why.

Language Box

Step 1. throw them away   give them to my siblings or relatives   sell them on a market app
keep them at home   donate to those who need them

Step 2. new clothes   towels   book covers   house decorations   art works   oven mittens

Grammar

Can / Could

I **can** swim.

He **could** ride a horse
when he was young.

An accident **can** happen.
An accident **could** happen.

Grammar Exercise

A *Rewrite the following sentences using the words in brackets.*

1. I speak French. [can]

_____

2. The rumor is true. [could]

_____

3. Kim plays soccer. [can]

_____

B *Put the words in the correct order to complete the following sentences.*

1. (the carpenter / can / a house / build).

_____

2. (a pop star / you / in / be / could / the future).

_____

3. (I / here / sit / could)?

_____

🎧 41

Do you sort waste? In Japan, there are a lot of sorting rules. Everyone says we should do it because recycling is thought to be a good thing for the environment. However, do you know where recyclable trash such as plastic bottles goes after we have sorted it? For many of us, the trash can is the end of the line for recycling.

5 Not all of our sorted waste is turned into other products. Let's think about where unrecycled waste goes. Some plastic waste that is not yet recycled is exported as "resources" to produce new products. However, this has become a problem. Large amounts of "resources" from Japan mainly travel to other Asian countries. The volume is too large for local workers to recycle. Also, it costs too much to recycle. Therefore, plastic material ends up being burned or put into the ground. In 10 other words, "resources" from Japan turn into trash, which damages the local environment.

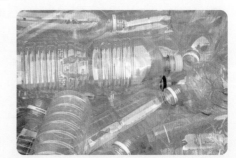

Our interests go only as far as what we see in our daily lives, but why not take an interest in what lies beyond that? You are sure to find new problems to solve to make the world 15 a better place.

Vocabulary Check

Fill in the blanks with words from the word box below.

1. A piece of paper (   ) easily.

2. The strong typhoon (   ) the forest.

3. Japan (   ) cars to other countries.

> exports   burns   damaged

Reading Comprehension

Read the article and choose the appropriate answer to the following questions.

1. Where do many unrecycled plastic bottles go?
   a. Schools
   b. Second-hand stores
   c. Asian countries
   d. Trash cans

2. What problem is mentioned in this article?
   a. Few people are interested in recycling.
   b. Not all plastic waste is recycled.
   c. Air pollution is a serious problem.
   d. It is difficult to sell used clothes.

3. According to the second paragraph, what does some plastic waste from Japan become in Asian countries?
   a. Resources
   b. Trash
   c. Clothes
   d. New plastic bottles

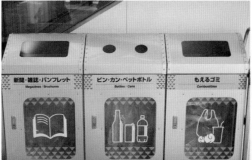

Writing

A *Put the words in the correct order to complete the following sentences.*

1. (Chloe / new clothes / three simple steps / makes / in).

   _____

2. (you / everything / have / to be / you need / an upcycler).

   _____

B *Fill in the blanks with your opinion and then write a short essay.*

Step 1 It is said that Japan has more household garbage than other countries. Make a list of several things you can do to reduce waste.

What I can do to reduce waste is _____.

Step 2 Of the things you listed in Step 1, which would be most effective for reducing waste?

_____ would be most effective.

Step 3 Write some more about effective ways to reduce waste.

Language Box

Step 1. refuse …   reduce …   reuse …   repurpose …   recycle …

....

Step 2. cans/bottles   paper   clothes   food   disposable products

Estate of the Arts

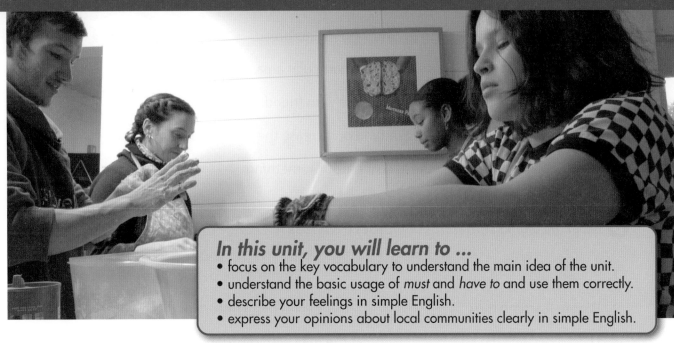

In this unit, you will learn to ...
- focus on the key vocabulary to understand the main idea of the unit.
- understand the basic usage of *must* and *have to* and use them correctly.
- describe your feelings in simple English.
- express your opinions about local communities clearly in simple English.

Warming Up

Choose your own answers to the following questions. Then ask your partner the questions.

1. What do you like to do in your free time?
   - ❑ Read books
   - ❑ Play games
   - ❑ Watch movies
   - ❑ Other (   )

2. Have you ever joined a club or community? If so, what kind?
   - ❑ Volunteering
   - ❑ Music
   - ❑ Sports
   - ❑ Other (   )

3. What type of food do you like the most?
   - ❑ Japanese
   - ❑ Chinese
   - ❑ Western
   - ❑ Other (   )

Watching   WEB動画 DVD CD 42

Watch the video and write down some words or phrases that you hear. Then share them with your friends.

making pizza

Vocabulary CD 43

A *Match the words and phrases below with the correct explanations (a – f).*

1. share   ———   **a.** to use something with others

2. add   ———   **b.** a person who makes bread

3. baker   ———   **c.** relating to a particular area

4. hang out   ———   **d.** to spend time with friends

5. base   ———   **e.** to combine or increase the amount of something

6. local   ———   **f.** the lowest part of something

B *Fill in the blanks with words or phrases from Task A. Change the word form if necessary.*

1. You should (   ) some more pepper if you want.

2. We are learning the (   ) history of this town.

3. I (   ) at the mall with my friend every day.

Listening Comprehension WEB動画 DVD CD 42

A *Watch the video again and write T if the statement is true or F if it is false.*

1. Many people spend their free time in Estate of the Arts.   ———

2. Ali does a workshop to earn money.   ———

3. Everyone enjoys making the pizzas in the workshop.   ———

4. Making pizza is a great way for everyone to spend their free time.   ———

B *Arrange the steps in making pizza in the order that they are mentioned in the video.*

Add the tomato sauce.

Put the pizza in the oven.

Put on the toppings and cheese.

Make the base.

_____ _____ _____ _____

Tips on Listening and Speaking 🎧 44

Strong Forms

Some function words sound very clear at the end of a sentence. By saying some function words more strongly, you can add emphasis to their meaning.

1. The pizzas are ready to come <u>out</u>.
2. I was surprised to know how expensive the computer <u>is</u>.
3. What an interesting story that <u>was</u>!

Dictation 🎧 45

Listen to the sentences and fill in the blanks.

1. He wants to show other people just how fun (   ) (   ).

2. Estate of the Arts is a place many people use in (   ) (   ) time.

3. Now, he has his (   ) kitchen at Estate of the Arts.

73

Retelling

Watch part of the video again and tell the story of the scene to your partner. You can use the keywords below.

Ali does a _____.
Keywords workshop, teach, young people

Ali enjoys _____.
Keywords hobby, so much

Ali wants to _____.
Keywords show, other people, how fun

Discussion

Fill in the blanks and exchange your ideas in pairs or small groups.

Step 1 When do you feel sad or uncomfortable?

I feel sad or uncomfortable when _____.

Step 2 What do you do when you feel sad or uncomfortable?

I usually _____.

Step 3 How do you get rid of your daily stress? Discuss in groups or pairs and share your opinions.

Language Box

Step 1. lose something   have many tasks to do   train is delayed
friend forgets his/her promise

....

Step 2. sleep a lot   sing in a loud voice   play video games   talk with friends   play sports
read books

Grammar

Must / Have to

You must finish your homework.

I have to finish my homework.

Grammar Exercise

A *Rewrite the following sentences using the words in brackets.*

1. I take the exam. [must]

   _____

2. The clerk doesn't do his work. [have to]

   _____

3. A kid waits for two hours. [have to]

   _____

B *Put the words in the correct order to complete the following sentences.*

1. (Leo / less money / spend / must).

   _____

2. (must / you / lies / tell / not).

   _____

3. (submit / to / the paper / the students / have).

   _____

🎵 46

Nowadays, there are endless opportunities for entertainment, and there is always something to do when we have a free day. Understanding what we like to do is important because it helps us manage the stress in our busy daily lives. Research suggests that doing something fun helps us relax and it is therefore good for both our physical and mental health.

5 Let's take a look at the benefits of doing what you like in your free time. If you enjoy communicating with other people, you can participate in group activities such as sports events or cooking workshops. This will help you become part of a community outside your school and will introduce you to new and exciting experiences. If you have a bad day, this can help you feel refreshed.

10 Some people, however, prefer to be less active. Perhaps they enjoy staying home and watching videos. Streaming services give us access to hundreds of movies. Watching movies makes it possible to "go" anywhere and "experience" whatever we want. If this sounds a little too passive, you could look into the background of the movie, imagine the characters' feelings, or even write your own review. In our daily lives, we have to work or study, but we also have to relax. Doing fun 15 things helps us to relax and gives us more energy to work or study.

Vocabulary Check

Fill in the blanks with words from the word box below.

1. Don't be (　　　　　　　　) when we're talking.

2. Our teacher explained to us the (　　　　　　　　) of speaking English.

3. Why don't you (　　　　　　　　) in some volunteer work this summer vacation?

participate　　passive　　benefits

Reading Comprehension

Read the article and choose the appropriate answer to the following questions.

1. According to the article, which of the following may help you relax?
   a. Working hard
   b. Watching movies
   c. Reading difficult magazines
   d. Spending time with your boss

2. What is one benefit of doing something fun?
   a. It saves time.
   b. It makes us feel relaxed.
   c. It helps us understand our friends' feelings.
   d. It helps us learn about society.

3. Which of the following activities would suit someone who enjoys communicating with others?
   a. Joining a baseball club
   b. Watching movies
   c. Writing book reviews
   d. Studying at home

77

Writing

A *Put the words in the correct order to complete the following sentences.*

1. (other people / is / it / to show / he wants / how fun).

   _____

2. (great way / your free time / what / spend / to / a)!

   _____

B *Fill in the blanks with your opinion and then write a short essay.*

Step 1 Local communities, clubs, or teams play an important role for many people. What kind of communities, clubs, or teams do you know about?

   I know _____, _____, and _____.

Step 2 What do you think is the good point about joining communities, clubs, or teams?

   I think the merit is _____.

Step 3 Write about the good points of communities, clubs, or teams.

Language Box

Step 1. soccer club   cooking workshop   language café   chorus group

Step 2. refresh   communicate with others   get to know each other   enjoy something new
    do different activities   be at ease   a wide age range   for free

UNIT 10

Plants Around Us

In this unit, you will learn to ...
- focus on the key vocabulary to understand the main idea of the unit.
- understand the basic usage of *if* and use it correctly.
- express your opinions regarding the environment based on information from the video or the reading.

Warming Up

Choose your own answers to the following questions. Then ask your partner the questions.

1. Have you ever grown plants? If so, what kind?
   - ❑ Flowers
   - ❑ Never
   - ❑ Vegetables
   - ❑ Other (   )

2. What vegetable do you like?
   - ❑ Tomatoes
   - ❑ Sweet potatoes
   - ❑ Cucumbers
   - ❑ Other (   )

3. When you choose a restaurant for lunch, what is the most important point for you?
   - ❑ Cost
   - ❑ Menu
   - ❑ Location
   - ❑ Other (   )

Watching WEB動画 📀DVD 💿CD 47

Watch the video and write down some words or phrases that you hear. Then share them with your friends.

an amazing garden

Vocabulary 🎧 48

A *Match the words and phrases below with the correct explanations (a – f).*

1. wild   _____   **a.** animal or plant living in a natural environment

2. facility   _____   **b.** to become fit for a new situation

3. adapt to   _____   **c.** a person who doesn't eat or use animal products

4. realize   _____   **d.** to understand clearly

5. vegan   _____   **e.** the upper outside part of a building

6. rooftop   _____   **f.** a place used for a particular purpose

B *Fill in the blanks with words or phrases from Task A. Change the word form if necessary.*

1. I found it hard at first to (   ) life at university.

2. I sometimes collect (   ) plants growing in the forest.

3. There is a nice sports (   ) in this city.

Listening Comprehension 💻 WEB動画 📀 DVD 🎧 CD 47

A *Watch the video again and write T if the statement is true or F if it is false.*

1. Kevin and John have a common in interest in growing their own food.   _____

2. In New York, people grow organic food on their rooftops.   _____

3. John has created a garden in an old factory, so it is hard for him to water plants.   _____

4. John doesn't throw away any food that he grows.   _____

B *Check the places which are mentioned in the video.*

☐ Bengaluru

☐ The Lake District

☐ Pacific Ocean

☐ London

☐ New York

Tips on Listening and Speaking 🎧 49

Linking (3)
The final sound of a word sometimes connects with the first sound of the next.

1. I would like to work with you.
2. Shake it off!
3. If it is safe, he cooks it.

Dictation 🎧 50

Listen to the sentences and fill in the blanks.

1. Kevin, Shweta, John, and Anastasia (   )
   (   ) very different places.

2. Their plants adapt to Bengaluru's (   )
   (   ).

3. Any food that's (   ) (   )
   is then composted.

Retelling

Watch part of the video again and tell the story of the scene to your partner. You can use the keywords below.

New York is _____.
Keywords busy, big, city

We can grow _____.
Keywords fresh, organic, New York

Even in a big city like New York, _____.
Keywords vegetables, plants, rooftop

Discussion

Fill in the blanks and exchange your ideas in pairs or small groups.

Step 1 Where do you think is the best place for you to grow plants?

I think _____ is the best place to grow them.

Step 2 Why did you choose that place in Step 1?

_____.

Step 3 Discuss in groups or pairs and evaluate each other's opinion.

Language Box

Step 1. garden   balcony   field   living room   my room

Step 2. easy to take care of   good environment   easy to adjust the temperature
grow under sunshine   have nutrients in the soil

Grammar

if

1. If + SV : an adverb clause

When we talk about something that might happen or be true, we use "if". This "if" introduces an adverb clause.

- If you have opinions, let me know.
- If you are tired, we will go home.
- I can lend you my pen if you forget yours.

2. If + SV : a noun clause

We can use "if" to mean the same as "whether." This "if" introduces a noun clause.

- I wonder if she knows the truth.
- He asked if I would like another cup of coffee.
- It is not certain if Tom can come tomorrow.

Grammar Exercise

A *Choose A if an adverb clause is included in the sentence, or N if a noun clause is included.*

1. (A / N) I will ask the teacher if I could leave class early.

2. (A / N) If it is sunny tomorrow, we will go on a picnic.

3. (A / N) Meg needs to practice hard if she wants to be a professional tennis player.

B *Put the words in the correct order to complete the following sentences.*

1. (rain tomorrow / I don't / will / if it / know).

   _____

2. (rains tomorrow / bring / an umbrella / if it / I will).

   _____

3. (our / we / the girl needs / help / will ask / if).

   _____

Reading

Midori City has decided to green the rooftops and walls of all elementary schools in the city. Students will grow vegetables such as
5 cucumbers on the schools' rooftops.

Mayor Yamada said that this measure is expected to reduce indoor temperatures and preserve the landscape. He added that growing vegetables is good for educating students about
10 food. The children will use the vegetables that they grow by cooking them in their home economics classes. Unused vegetables will be sold in the summer festival this year. The Mayor expects that more and more students will understand the importance of food by learning how to
15 grow vegetables and prepare meals.

In addition to playing a big role in the children's education, this greening plan is also very important from the point of view of environmental preservation. Mayor Yamada intends to promote it further in the future.

Comments

Ken: I live in a different city, but my school is also greening its rooftops. It certainly feels cooler but taking care of them and cleaning them every day is hard work.

Mary: They also cost a lot of money because we have to replant them every year. Is this really the best way?

Tom: I hear vegetables on rooftops are effective against global warming. The cost is not huge, so we should do more.

Vocabulary Check

Fill in the blanks with words from the word box below.

1. We should (   ) World Heritage sites while welcoming tourists.

2. My brother and I (   ) to study abroad next year.

3. This app is (   ) for taking notes.

preserve   effective   intend

Reading Comprehension

Read the article and choose the appropriate answer to the following questions.

1. What did the mayor mention about the greening project?
   a. The cost
   b. The effects
   c. The necessity
   d. An opposite opinion

2. What will happen to unused vegetables?
   a. They will be given away.
   b. They will be thrown away.
   c. They will be eaten by animals.
   d. They will go on sale.

3. Who thinks that greening rooftops and walls is too expensive?
   a. The Mayor
   b. Ken
   c. Mary
   d. Tom

Writing

A *Put the words in the correct order to complete the following sentences.*

1. (delicious food / them / the garden / around / all year / gives).

    _____

2. (John / a garden / so much / loves plants / that / he created).

    _____

B *Fill in the blanks with your opinion and then write a short essay.*

Step 1 What kind of greenery is there in your city?

    There is/are _____.

Step 2 What do you think about the amount of greenery in your city?

    I think _____.

Step 3 Describe the greening situation in your city.

Language Box

Step 1. flower beds   roadside trees   forest   fields   greening walls   greening rooftops

Step 2. enough   not enough   parks should be greened   find everywhere
          decreasing year by year   too little to notice

Farmers Market

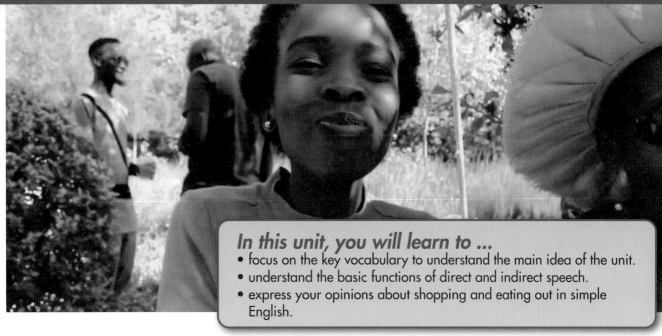

In this unit, you will learn to ...
- focus on the key vocabulary to understand the main idea of the unit.
- understand the basic functions of direct and indirect speech.
- express your opinions about shopping and eating out in simple English.

Warming Up

Choose your own answers to the following questions. Then ask your partner the questions.

1. What vegetable do you eat most often?
   ❑ Potatoes   ❑ Tomatoes
   ❑ Onions   ❑ Other (   )

2. Where do you usually go shopping?
   ❑ Shopping districts   ❑ Supermarkets
   ❑ Shopping malls   ❑ Other (   )

3. What do you know about South Africa?
   ❑ Sports   ❑ Food
   ❑ History   ❑ Places

Watching WEB動画 🖥 DVD CD 52

Watch the video and write down some words or phrases that you hear. Then share them with your friends.

market

Vocabulary

🎧 53

A *Match the words below with the correct explanations (a – f).*

1. selection _____ a. very good, attractive, enjoyable, etc.

2. freshly _____ b. to get liquid from something by pressing it

3. squeeze _____ c. recently made or done

4. definitely _____ d. something small eaten between meals

5. snack _____ e. without any doubt

6. fantastic _____ f. the careful choice of a particular person or thing

B *Fill in the blanks with words from Task A. Change the word form if necessary.*

1. I ( ) need a day off.

2. The children eat their ( ) around three o'clock.

3. I had a ( ) meal at the newly opened restaurant.

Listening Comprehension

WEB動画 📀 DVD 🎧 CD 52

A *Watch the video again and write T if the statement is true or F if it is false.*

1. First, Bokang goes to a sandwich stall. _____

2. Bokang chooses a chicken option for her sandwich. _____

3. For a snack, Bokang has some fried potatoes. _____

4. Bokang says you should go to a market in Sandton. _____

B *Check the things Bokang eats and drinks in the video.*

☐ beef　　☐ chicken　　☐ spaghetti　　☐ sandwich

☐ juice

☐ potatoes

☐ sausage

☐ tomato

Tips on Listening and Speaking 🎧 54

Weakening (2)
A weakening sometimes happens at the end of content words.

1. She wants to buy a new <u>camera</u>.
2. I like to spend time with my <u>family</u>.
3. The plants need <u>watering</u>.

Dictation 🎧 55

Listen to the sentences and fill in the blanks.

1. My channel is called "The B (   )" and I share parts of my life.

2. I was thirsty, so my (   ) (   ) was a juice stand called Impressed.

3. This one is (   ) one of my favorites.

Retelling WEB動画 🖥️ 💿 DVD

Watch part of the video again and tell the story of the scene to your partner. You can use the keywords below.

This is _____.
Keywords market, big, food, selection

There is _____.
Keywords people, enjoy, meal

I'm going to _____.
Keywords eat, drink, delicious

Discussion

Fill in the blanks and exchange your ideas in pairs or small groups.

Step 1 Where do you like to shop?

I like to go to _____.

Step 2 What do you like about that store?

I like _____.

Step 3 Ask your partner about their choice of store and discuss the similarities and differences.

Language Box

Step 1. supermarket   convenience store   shopping district   market   shopping mall
department store   small shop

Step 2. close to home   good selection   cheap   reasonable   kind/friendly staff
good atmosphere

Grammar

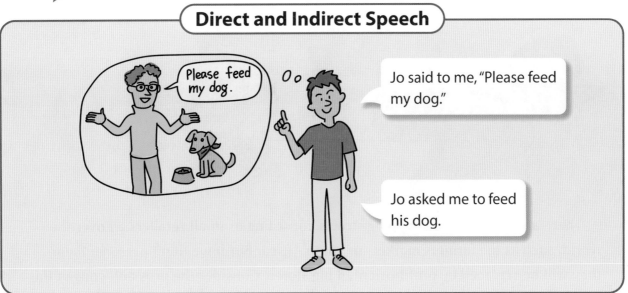

Direct and Indirect Speech

Jo said to me, "Please feed my dog."

Jo asked me to feed his dog.

Grammar Exercise

A *Choose the correct answer to complete the following sentences.*

1. The shop clerk (said / told), "It's a gift from those people over there."

2. The wife (said / told) her husband, "You said the same thing yesterday."

3. The teacher told the students to submit the homework assigned three days (before / ago).

B *Put the words in the correct order to complete the following sentences.*

1. (the patient / told / the doctor / would be difficult / the treatment / that).

   _____

2. (away / the hunter / "Stay / said, / from here.")

   _____

3. (the police officer / the suspect / asked / her advice / follow / to).

   _____

Reading

🎧 56

There are markets and shopping streets consisting of small retailers all over the world, such as the farmers markets in South Africa. But if we don't preserve them, they will be replaced by profit-oriented big stores. Consider the pros and cons of this based on the following opinion by a Japanese university student.

5   I recently visited my hometown and was surprised to see that my favorite shopping street had been completely shuttered. It feels incredibly lonely, leaving a hole in my heart.

In the shopping street, there was a close connection between the shopkeepers and me. The shopkeepers and customers were mostly locals. That's why they
10 cherished the community and its people. However, I feel that recent part-time workers at large chain stores lack a connection with local people.

People prefer to buy goods at a lower price because of the tough economy. We can do this at large chain stores. Also, it appears that the law regulating large stores has been abolished, making it easier for them to establish their presence.
15   Because of globalization, the next stage will be that large Japanese stores might be replaced by foreign mega-stores. It's a worrying possibility that looms on the horizon. The day may come soon.

Vocabulary Check

Fill in the blanks with words from the word box below.

1. My parents always (   ) their memories of my childhood.

2. (   ) buy some vegetables and cook them themselves here.

3. A police officer is always there to (   ) traffic.

regulate	customers	cherished

Reading Comprehension

Read the article and choose the appropriate answer to the following questions.

1. What did the people in the shopping street cherish?
   a. Communities
   b. Their products
   c. Shutters
   d. Lower prices

2. What is the attraction of big chain stores?
   a. Quality
   b. Low prices
   c. Connection between people
   d. Location

3. Who is likely to benifit from global competition?
   a. Shopping streets
   b. Big chain stores
   c. Foreign mega-stores
   d. Shopping malls

Writing

A *Put the words in the correct order to complete the following sentences.*

1. (I / find / something / decided / to / to eat).

   _____

2. (that / delicious sandwiches / sells / there / a stall / is).

   _____

B *Fill in the blanks with your opinion and then write a short essay.*

Step 1 When do you want to eat at a local restaurant?

   I want to eat there when _____.

Step 2 When do you want to eat at a chain restaurant?

   I want to eat there when _____.

Step 3 Write about which kind of restaurant, a local restaurant or a chain restaurant, you would like to run.

Language Box

Step 1. local ingredients   communication   sightseeing   save money   eat with friends
eat with family

Step 2. unfamiliar place   trendy food   everyday food   eat expensive food   go on a date
don't have time

Party Planning

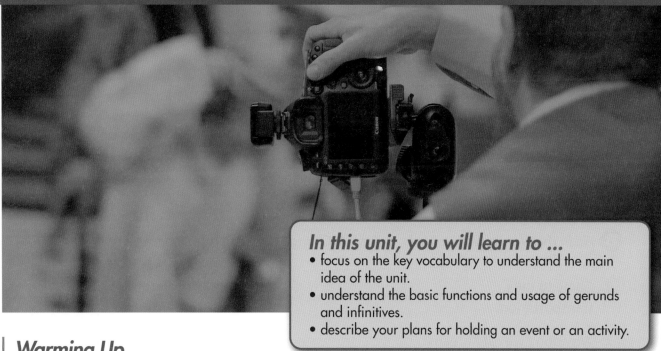

In this unit, you will learn to ...
- focus on the key vocabulary to understand the main idea of the unit.
- understand the basic functions and usage of gerunds and infinitives.
- describe your plans for holding an event or an activity.

Warming Up

Choose your own answers to the following questions. Then ask your partner the questions.

1. What kind of party have you attended?
   - ❏ A birthday party
   - ❏ A wedding party
   - ❏ A New Year's Day party
   - ❏ Other (   )

2. Have you ever planned an event?
   - ❏ Yes, often
   - ❏ Yes, rarely
   - ❏ Yes, sometimes
   - ❏ No, never

3. What kind of party would you like to attend in the future?
   - ❏ A wedding party
   - ❏ A company party
   - ❏ A home party
   - ❏ Other (   )

Watching   WEB動画 🖥 📀 DVD 💿 CD 57

Watch the video and write down some words or phrases that you hear. Then share them with your friends.

> party

Vocabulary 🎧 58

Ⓐ *Match the words below with the correct explanations (a – f).*

1. formal _____
2. decor _____
3. circus _____
4. venue _____
5. barbecue _____
6. elegant _____

a. the location where an event takes place
b. a traveling group that performs acrobatics, etc.
c. beautiful, attractive, or graceful
d. very polite and used in official situations
e. an outdoor meal with grilled meat, seafood, vegetables, and so on
f. the way that the inside of a house is decorated

Ⓑ *Fill in the blanks with words from Task A. Change the word form if necessary.*

1. Come to the (   ) of the annual conference by public transportation.

2. Why don't we eat Korean (   ) in my garden?

3. My sister likes the interior (   ) of the restaurant.

Listening Comprehension WEB動画 DVD 🎧 57

Ⓐ *Watch the video again and write T if the statement is true or F if it is false.*

1. Hugo is going to have a birthday party. _____
2. Hugo wants the party to be elegant. _____
3. The party is going to be in spring. _____
4. At the party there will be 300 guests. _____

Ⓑ *Put the items on Hugo's to-do list in order.*

Decide on a date and time

Choose the theme

Choose the food   Invite the guests

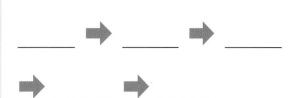

Choose the venue

Tips on Listening and Speaking   🎧 59

Elision (2)
On some occasions, English speakers leave out a sound.

1. When you wake up in the morning, say "Good morning."
2. I just called to say "I miss you."
3. An old man with white hair gave me a kind word.

Dictation   🎧 60

Listen to the sentences and fill in the blanks.

1. Somewhere that is just (   ). Then, he has a great idea for the (   ) venue.

2. Hugo started (   ) own business.

3. Hugo is sure (   ) find the right place.

97

Retelling

Watch part of the video again and tell the story of the scene to your partner. You can use the keywords below.

A man and a woman _____.
Keywords plan, party

A woman is _____.
Keywords stand, write, whiteboard

They need to _____.
Keywords decide, venue, theme, food

Discussion

Fill in the blanks and exchange your ideas in pairs or small groups.

Step 1 If you have a birthday party, what will you prepare?

I will prepare _____.

Step 2 Who would you like to invite to the party?

I want to invite _____ to the party.

Step 3 Ask your partner about their party and give them advice on how to make their party better.

Language Box

Step 1. sushi   pizza   drumsticks (chicken legs)   salad   desserts   cakes   soft drinks
card games   balloons   party favors

....

Step 2. parents   grandparents   relatives   friends   acquaintances   celebrities
teachers   politicians

Grammar

Gerunds and Infinitives

PAST ◄━━━━━━━━━━━━━━━━━━━━► FUTURE

- My father gave up playing golf.
- I've finished talking with the guests.
- I remember giving him a gift.

- I want to see your family.
- I decided to go to the party.
- Remember to give him a gift.

Grammar Exercise

A *Choose the correct answer to complete the following sentences.*

1. The family expected (to welcome / welcoming) 100 people.

2. The kindergarten children enjoyed (singing / to sing) with their classmates.

3. The truck driver avoided (going / to go) through narrow roads.

B *Put the words in the correct order to complete the following sentences.*

1. (a sports event / decided / organize / the mayor / to).

_____

2. (my father likes / the guitar / playing / the garden / in).

_____

3. (forgot / door / the / to lock / the professor / classroom).

_____

UNIT 1 UNIT 2 UNIT 3 UNIT 4 UNIT 5 UNIT 6 UNIT 7 UNIT 8 UNIT 9 UNIT 10 UNIT 11 **UNIT 12** UNIT 13 UNIT 14 UNIT 15

🎧 61

When planning a party or trip, deciding when to schedule it is one of the biggest concerns. This may not be a problem if the event involves only students. However, if it involves family members who have various jobs, parents may have to make their children skip classes to go on a trip when the parents are

5 free. Here are some opinions on this matter.

Miguel

I am against parents making their children skip classes because parents have a duty to provide education to their children, and family trips would deprive children of their right to receive education. In school, children learn things that will be important in their

15 lives. If that opportunity is taken away, children may miss out on things that will be important for their future employment and social life.

Kenta

I am in favor of it because family trips

20 offer unique learning experiences that can only be gained through such trips. By thinking of it as one form of education, we can foster children with various viewpoints. I recently

25 came across a newly coined word, "learcation," which is a combination of "learning" and "vacation." While we need to think about the gap between rich and poor, I find it to be an interesting approach.

Vocabulary Check

Fill in the blanks with words from the word box below.

1. The teacher (   ) the students of enjoyment of the holiday.

2. I (   ) a lot of weight.

3. Mistakes will (   ) our development.

gained	foster	deprived

Reading Comprehension

Read the article and choose the appropriate answer to the following questions.

1. Based on the passage, what is the biggest concern when planning a party or trip?
   a. Location
   b. Schedule
   c. Members
   d. Learning

2. According to Miguel, what must parents provide for their children?
   a. Employment
   b. Education
   c. Meals
   d. Family trips

3. According to Kenta, what are unique learning experiences?
   a. Family trips
   b. School education
   c. Club activities
   d. Cram schools

Writing

A *Put the words in the correct order to complete the following sentences.*

1. (really / themselves / they / enjoy).

_____

2. (going to have / next party / is / when / his / Hugo)?

_____

B *Fill in the blanks with your opinion and then write a short essay.*

Step 1 What is the most important point when planning a trip?

The most important point for me is _____.

Step 2 What is the reason behind your opinion?

The reason behind my opinion is _____.

Step 3 Write some advice to someone planning a trip.

Language Box

Step 1.	destination season schedule money members hotels meals transportation luggage language
Step 2.	enjoy difficult experience anxiety rain new things save money translation tour guides

War on Waste

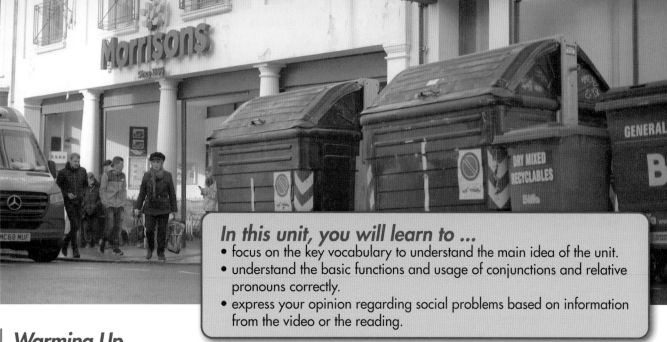

In this unit, you will learn to ...
• focus on the key vocabulary to understand the main idea of the unit.
• understand the basic functions and usage of conjunctions and relative pronouns correctly.
• express your opinion regarding social problems based on information from the video or the reading.

Warming Up

Choose your own answers to the following questions. Then ask your partner the questions.

1. Have you thrown away food at home? If so, what kind?
   ❑ Meat   ❑ Vegetables/Fruits
   ❑ Rice   ❑ Other (   )

2. Which of the following have you done to reduce food waste?
   ❑ Buy non-standard products   ❑ Buy appropriate amounts of food
   ❑ Prepare appropriate amounts of food   ❑ Other (   )

3. Which of the following have you donated to?
   ❑ Poor children   ❑ Homeless people
   ❑ Disaster areas   ❑ Other (   )

Watching   WEB動画 🖥️ DVD 💿 CD 62

Watch the video and write down some words or phrases that you hear. Then share them with your friends.

> *waste*

Vocabulary 🎧 63

A *Match the words and phrases below with the correct explanations (a – f).*

1. found   _____   **a.** a person who controls or manages a company

2. director   _____   **b.** to start something such as a company

3. junk food   _____   **c.** a large number or amount of something

4. bin   _____   **d.** a skilled cook

5. chef   _____   **e.** a container for putting waste in

6. load   _____   **f.** food that is high in calories but low in nutrition

B *Fill in the blanks with words or phrases from Task A. Change the word form if necessary.*

1. My cousin will (   ) a school for poor children.

2. The previous (   ) of the financial program resigned, so we hired a new one.

3. His dream is to cook as a (   ) in a big hotel.

Listening Comprehension 📺WEB動画 📀DVD 🎧 62

A *Watch the video again and write T if the statement is true or F if it is false.*

1. Every morning, the Real Junk Food Project gets waste food from supermarkets.   _____

2. If nobody takes the food, the supermarket puts it in the bin.   _____

3. Paul is a well-paid chef.   _____

4. Lots of people come to the project and enjoy food.   _____

B *Put the following sentences in the order they appear in the video.*

The founding director is introduced.

Volunteers cook a big meal for the community.

104

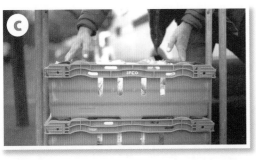

The team gets food from supermarkets.

People come to get food.

People enjoy the food together.

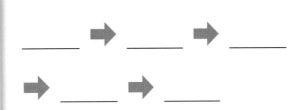

Tips on Listening and Speaking 🎧 64

Weakening (3)
Weakening sometimes happens between two closely related words.

1. My favorite sandwich is ham <u>and</u> eggs.
2. You believe <u>that</u> it is untrue.
3. The teacher wants <u>you</u> to come here.

Dictation 🎧 65

Listen to the sentences and fill in the blanks.

1. Lots of different people come (   ) enjoy
   the food together.

2. (   ) they (   ) take it, it
   goes in the bin.

3. Adam started the Junk Food Project (   )
   he hates seeing good food go to waste.

Retelling

WEB動画 🖥 💿DVD

Watch part of the video again and tell the story of the scene to your partner. You can use the keywords below.

Cities, cafés, and restaurants _____.
Keywords need, lot, food

They also _____.
Keywords create, waste

The team _____.
Keywords get, food, supermarket

Discussion

Fill in the blanks and exchange your ideas in pairs or small groups.

Step 1 What parts of vegetables do you throw away?

I throw away _____.

Step 2 Think of dishes you can make using the vegetables you mentioned in Step 1.

I can make _____.

Step 3 Ask your partner about their dishes and decide the most delicious one.

Language Box

Step 1. vegetable stems   seeds   vegetable scraps   discolored   parts eaten by insects

....

Step 2. soup   curry   stew   gratin   salad   pizza   barbecue

Grammar

Conjunctions / Relative Pronouns

A Conjunctions

① _____ S1 + V1 _____ , and/but/or _____ S2 + V2 _____

② _____ S + V _____ when/that/if _____ S' + V' _____

① Get plenty of rest, and you'll feel better soon.

② We often had barbecues in the garden when I was a child.

B Relative Pronouns

③ _____ S + V _____ noun that _____ S' + V' _____
↳ Necessary Information

④ _____ S + V _____ noun , which _____ S' + V' _____
↳ Extra Information

③ The two classes that I'm taking were canceled last week.

④ The two classes, which I'm taking, were canceled last week.

Grammar Exercise

A *Choose the correct answer to complete the following sentences.*

1. You said (that / which) he was selfish.

2. I cooked dinner with the fish (that / when) the neighbors gave to me.

3. The photographer took pictures of the actor (which / who) won an award.

B *Put the words in the correct order to complete the following sentences.*

1. (by the coach / the theory that / with / agreed / had been developed / the athlete).

_____

2. (that / by / the singer arranged / was composed / a song / a famous composer).

_____

3. (prefer companies / but / not only themselves / also society / people / that benefit).

Reading

🎵 66

      "Children's Cafeterias" are places that provide free or cheap meals for children from low-income families. There are many children in Japan who need this kind of support. Because getting enough good-quality food is necessary for a happy life, some NPOs run children's cafeterias to enrich children's lives through enjoyable meals.

5   It is a sad fact that much food is thrown away. In using such food, children's cafeterias also play an important role in reducing food waste. These cafeterias rely on donations and volunteers. They receive donations such as vegetables from local farmers. Volunteer staff cook and serve the meals and enjoy them with the children.

      If you would like to make a difference in children's lives through food, you can
10 become a volunteer. Just contact some children's cafeterias in your area and enjoy helping the children!

Vocabulary Check

Fill in the blanks with words from the word box below.

1. The company (   ) financial support for children in poverty.

2. Don't live beyond your (   ).

3. My friend is planning to make a generous (   ) because he is unmarried and has no children.

| income | provides | donation |

Reading Comprehension

Read the article and choose the appropriate answer to the following questions.

1. In what way do the cafeterias enrich children's lives?
   a. Through meals
   b. Through donations
   c. Through education
   d. Through medical care

2. How are the activities of this type of NPO supported?
   a. By parents
   b. By donations
   c. By the government
   d. By rich people

3. What can we do to get more information?
   a. Contact the organization
   b. Attend a meeting
   c. Donate something
   d. Report on something

Writing

A *Put the words in the correct order to complete the following sentences.*

1. (a big meal / cooking / the community / they're / for).

   _____

2. (can take / everybody / need / the food / they).

   _____

B *Fill in the blanks with your opinion and then write a short essay.*

Step 1 What do you think causes food waste?

   I think it is _____ .

Step 2 What can we do to prevent this?

   We can _____ .

Step 3 Describe ways to improve food waste.

Language Box

Step 1. leftovers   buy too much   make too much   mass production   remove too much
   overly strict expiration date

Step 2. eat all   appropriate amount   grow your own vegetables   not to make too much
   not to remove too much

Layla's Vegan Café

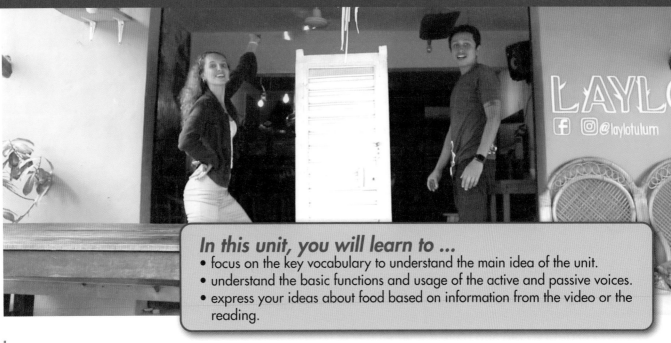

In this unit, you will learn to ...
- focus on the key vocabulary to understand the main idea of the unit.
- understand the basic functions and usage of the active and passive voices.
- express your ideas about food based on information from the video or the reading.

Warming Up

Choose your own answers to the following questions. Then ask your partner the questions.

1. What kind of food do you like?
   - ❏ Meat
   - ❏ Fish
   - ❏ Vegetables
   - ❏ Other (   )

2. If you were the owner of a restaurant, where would you want it to be located?
   - ❏ Near a station
   - ❏ Near a shopping mall
   - ❏ Near a beach
   - ❏ Other (   )

3. Have you ever eaten vegan food?
   - ❏ No, never
   - ❏ Yes, often
   - ❏ Yes, but only once
   - ❏ Other (   )

Watching

WEB動画 🖥 💿 DVD CD 67

Watch the video and write down some words or phrases that you hear. Then share them with your friends.

vegan

Vocabulary 🎧 68

A *Match the word below with the correct explanations (a – f).*

1. dairy   _____
2. prepare   _____
3. include   _____
4. sore   _____
5. planet   _____
6. coast   _____

a. to contain
b. painful
c. milk, cheese, and other milk products
d. to make someone ready to do something
e. land near the sea
f. a big round object that goes around a star

B *Fill in the blanks with words from Task A. Change the word form if necessary.*

1. We should (   ) for the party.

2. Their work (   ) cleaning the rooms.

3. I caught a cold and have a severe (   ) throat.

Listening Comprehension WEB動画 📀 DVD 🎧 CD 67

A *Watch the video again and write T if the statement is true or F if it is false.*

1. There are a lot of people on the Caribbean coast of Mexico.   _____

2. Both Lalo and Layla are from Mexico.   _____

3. Lalo and Layla buy the ingredients they need every day.   _____

4. The number of people who are becoming vegan is increasing.   _____

B *Check the items that are included on Laylo's menu in the video.*

☐ juice containing **tomato**   ☐ juice containing **carrot**   ☐ juice containing **greens**

☐ a beetroot burger   ☐ a cheeseburger   ☐ a potato and avocado burger

Tips on Listening and Speaking   🎵 69

Assimilation (3)
Sometimes two different sounds combine into one sound.

1. I miss you.
2. My brother will send you an email.
3. Nice to meet you.

Dictation   🎵 70

Listen to the sentences and fill in the blanks.

1. It's good for your skin (   ) (   ) eyes.

2. With beautiful beaches, good weather (   ) (   ) (   ),
   and not too many people to share it with.

3. She decided it was just the right place to start (   ) (   ) vegan
   business.

113

Retelling

Watch part of the video again and tell the story of the scene to your partner. You can use the keywords below.

Layla and Lalo _____ .
> **Keywords** both, vegan

Vegan people _____ .
> **Keywords** eat, vegetables, beans

Layla and Lalo know that if we all eat less meat and dairy, we'll _____ .
> **Keywords** help, climate change

Discussion

Fill in the blanks and exchange your ideas in pairs or small groups.

Step 1 If you were the owner of a restaurant, who would be your target customers?

I think _____ would be the target customers of my restaurant.

Step 2 What service or menu would be necessary in your restaurant?

_____ is/are necessary in the restaurant.

Step 3 Share your ideas within groups or pairs.

Language Box

Step 1. students   business people   people with their pets   people with babies   vegetarians   elderly people   families

....

Step 2. colorful sweets   quick service   efficient service   cheap menu   open space   toys

114

Grammar

Grammar Exercise

A *Change the following sentences into the passive voice or active voice.*

1. I held this meeting.

   _____

2. The ball was kicked by him.

   _____

3. Aya used this pen.

   _____

B *Put the words in the correct order to complete the following sentences.*

1. (their mother / the children / loved / are / by).

   _____

2. (in / this bridge / 2005 / was / built).

   _____

3. (English / spoken / in / is / Australia).

   _____

115

🎧 71

Maybe you know the words "vegetarian" and "vegan." But do you know the difference between them?

Vegetarians are people who do not eat meat. Their reasons for this include looking after their health, protecting the
5　environment, showing respect for other living creatures, or following religious rules.

All vegetarians eat plant-based foods such as vegetables and beans. Depending on the person, they may or may not eat dairy products, eggs, and fish. For example, "lacto-vegetarians"
10　may eat dairy products but not fish or meat. Vegetarians decide what to eat and what not to eat depending on their own values.

People who eat only plant-based foods are called vegans. Some vegans do not even use clothing or household items that are made from animal products. Moreover, stricter
15　vegans try to find out whether products have been tested on animals. If so, they will refuse to use them.

It is important for us to understand and respect the diversity of choices. In recent years, an increasing number of Japanese restaurants have included vegetarian items on their
20　menus. However, such menus are still far from common in Japan. Consideration is needed so that as many people as possible can enjoy their daily meals.

VEGAN

Vocabulary Check

Fill in the blanks with words from the word box below.

1. We (   ) good manners in this community.

2. "Vegetarian" is a word in (   ) use.

3. I (   ) to change my job.

common	value	decided

Reading Comprehension

Read the article and choose the appropriate answer to the following questions.

1. Which statement is true about vegans?
   a. They do not have pets.
   b. They do not eat animal products.
   c. They do not eat nuts.
   d. They do not live in wooden houses.

2. What is a difference between vegetarians and vegans?
   a. Some vegetarians eat fish.
   b. Some vegetarians do not eat cabbages.
   c. Some vegans wear animal fur.
   d. Some vegans do not wear cotton shirts.

3. What is necessary for everyone to enjoy their daily meals in comfort?
   a. Cooking meals by ourselves
   b. Eating only vegetables
   c. Using local vegetables in restaurants
   d. Understanding people's values

117

Writing

A *Put the words in the correct order to complete the following sentences.*

1. (it / time / is / to / the food / prepare).

   _____

2. (more / becoming / vegan / are / and more / people).

   _____

B *Fill in the blanks with your opinion and then write a short essay.*

Step 1 What are some dishes that vegans cannot eat as they are usually prepared?

_____ , _____ , and _____ are.

Step 2 If you could prepare one of the dishes that you wrote in Step 1 for vegans, how would you prepare it?

I would make _____ using _____ instead of _____ .

Step 3 Write about the vegan menu that you would like to make.

Language Box

Step 1. hamburger   steak   fried pork cutlet   beef stew   spaghetti with meat sauce

Step 2. beans   vegetables   tofu   rice   nuts   wheat   grain   fruits   soy milk
beef   pork   chicken   fish   eggs   milk

Climbing Buddies

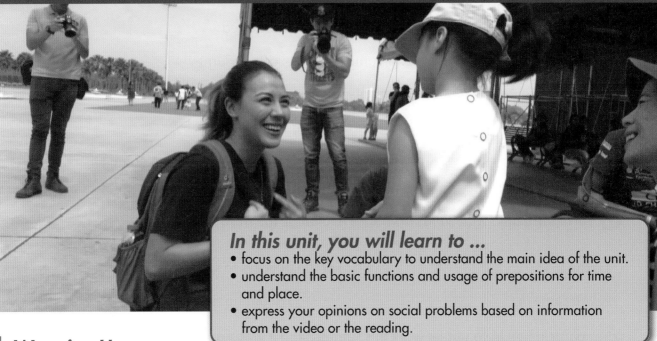

In this unit, you will learn to ...
- focus on the key vocabulary to understand the main idea of the unit.
- understand the basic functions and usage of prepositions for time and place.
- express your opinions on social problems based on information from the video or the reading.

Warming Up

Choose your own answers to the following questions. Then ask your partner the questions.

1. Have you ever climbed a mountain? If so, which one?
   - ❏ Mt. Fuji
   - ❏ A local mountain in my hometown
   - ❏ Mt. Takao
   - ❏ Other ( )

2. Have you ever done volunteer work?
   - ❏ Yes, once
   - ❏ No, never
   - ❏ Yes, often
   - ❏ Other ( )

3. What kind of volunteer work are you interested in?
   - ❏ Picking up trash
   - ❏ Activities for the handicapped
   - ❏ Activities for children
   - ❏ Other ( )

Watching WEB動画 📺 DVD CD 72

Watch the video and write down some words or phrases that you hear. Then share them with your friends.

climb a mountain

Vocabulary 🎧 73

A *Match the words below with the correct explanations (a – f).*

1. base _____   **a.** an important job

2. sight _____   **b.** something that is required

3. needs _____   **c.** an unusual and exciting journey

4. experience _____   **d.** the place you start from or return to

5. adventure _____   **e.** a thing that you see

6. mission _____   **f.** knowledge that you have gained from doing an activity

B *Fill in the blanks with words from Task A. Change the word form if necessary.*

1. The (   ) of the police is to save citizens.

2. We came in (   ) of our hometown.

3. I participated in volunteer work this summer and it was a great
(   ) for me.

Listening Comprehension 🖥️ 📀DVD 🎧72

A *Watch the video again and write T if the statement is true or F if it is false.*

1. In Bangkok, winters are extremely cold. _____

2. Carla's climbing buddy is a child with special needs. _____

3. Even though San San doesn't speak, Carla and San San can communicate in different ways. _____

4. It took more than five hours to climb the mountain. _____

B *Arrange the main ideas in the order that they are mentioned in the video.*

a

Carla and San San communicated with the help of San San's mother.

Carla felt very close to San San and will miss her.

Carla decided to carry San San.

Tips on Listening and Speaking 🔊 74

Assimilation (4)
Some speech sounds change and become more similar to the sound just before or after them.

1. Carla is a TV prese<u>nt</u>er.
2. Carla wa<u>nt</u>ed to go to Chatuchak.
3. The top of the mou<u>nta</u>in was in sight.

Dictation 🔊 75

Listen to the sentences and fill in the blanks.

1. On the (　　　　　　) of January last year, she arrived in Bangkok, the
   (　　　　　　) of Thailand.

2. San San (　　　　　) (　　　　　　　) walk as much as possible.

3. They climbed (　　　　　　) three hours, and finally the top (　　　　　　) the
   mountain was (　　　　　) sight.

121

Retelling

WEB動画 🖥️ 💿DVD

Watch part of the video again and tell the story of the scene to your partner. You can use the keywords below.

After the climb, Carla _____.
Keywords felt, close, San San

_____ for Carla.
Keywords saying goodbye, easy

This climbing _____.
Keywords special, experience

Discussion

Fill in the blanks and exchange your ideas in pairs or small groups.

Step 1 If you were to climb a mountain, what do you think would be the most important thing?

I think _____.

Step 2 If you were the San San's climbing buddy, what would you do to support her?

I would _____.

Step 3 Share your opinions within groups or pairs.

Language Box

Step 1. understand the situation quickly   adapt to the environment
control your body temperature   ensure safety

....

Step 2. take as much rest as possible   talk to her a lot
study her condition before climbing   learn hand signs

Grammar

Prepositions for Time and Place

① from ② to ③ for ④ on ⑤ at ⑥ in

- I had to wait **for** two hours to travel **from** Tokyo **to** Kyoto.
  ③Time   ①Place   ②Place

- Put the decorations **on** the ceiling and desks.
  ④Place

- You should be **in** the classroom **at** noon.
  ⑥Place   ⑤Time

Grammar Exercise

A *Fill in the blanks to complete the following sentences.*

1. I am waiting (　　　　) the bus stop.

2. The professor put his books (　　　　) the table.

3. We met a man (　　　　) night.

B *Put the words in the correct order to complete the following sentences.*

1. (phone / on / talked / my brother / the).

   _____

2. (I / in / will / be / ten minutes / back).

   _____

3. (is / wine / grapes / made / from).

   _____

Reading

🎧 76

   Recently, thanks to developments in technology, our daily lives are becoming more comfortable and convenient. This is especially true for visually handicapped people.

   It is now extremely common for people to communicate with text messages in messenger apps. You might think that such tools are not used by visually handicapped people. Not so long
5 ago, this was true. However, in recent years, the situation has changed.

   With the development of voice recognition technology and apps that can turn text into speech, it is no longer difficult for visually handicapped people to use written communication apps in real time.

   Of course, they still face problems. Current technology still does not recognize visual
10 elements such as emojis. This makes it more difficult to communicate emotions. Also, it may be difficult to hear messages in noisy places. But even though there are problems, communication options have expanded. New apps have made it easier for visually handicapped people to communicate with texts. They are also useful for people who are not good at using computers or smartphones. In addition, they help people who have problems with their hands or fingers.
15   It is important to listen to the voices of people who face difficulties. This will help us to develop useful new technology in the future.

Vocabulary Check

Fill in the blanks with words from the word box below.

1. Smartphones are one of the most important (   ) in our lives.

2. (   ) of the difficulties faced by handicapped people is important.

3. Buds will (   ) into flowers.

recognition   tools   turn

Reading Comprehension

Read the article and choose the appropriate answer to the following questions.

1. How has technology benefited visually handicapped people?
   a. Recording their own voice to send messages
   b. Chatting online instantly
   c. Taking photos easily
   d. Sending text messages using emoji

2. What is a problem when visually handicapped people use messenger apps?
   a. Using them in a crowded station
   b. Buying stickers
   c. Noticing replies
   d. Sending messages quickly

3. How can we understand where technology needs more development?
   a. By using voice recognition technology
   b. By communicating with engineers
   c. By researching ways of using messenger apps
   d. By understanding the needs of people who have difficulties in daily life

Writing

A *Put the words in the correct order to complete the following sentences.*

1. (in / San San / ways / different / communicates).

   _____

2. (more team photos / time / for / there / was).

   _____

B *Fill in the blanks with your opinion and then write a short essay.*

Step 1 Who would benefit from self-driving private cars?

   I think _____ would benefit.

Step 2 What functions would be important for the people you wrote in Step 1?

   I think _____ would be important.

Step 3 Write about your ideal self-driving private car.

Language Box

Step 1. visually handicapped people   people who have disability in their fingers or hands
   elderly people   people who drive a long distance   people who occasionally drive a car

Step 2. know the color of traffic lights   understand the situation in front of the car
   give directions using your voice   drive using only your hands/legs

Appendix

Useful Expressions for Discussions

Giving your thoughts/opinions

- ☐ I believe that it is a good idea (to do something) because …
- ☐ I don't think that it is a good idea (that we send it to them) because …
- ☐ In my opinion, it is not important (to do something) because …
- ☐ My opinion is (that we should look after them) because …
- ☐ It was interesting to know that …
- ☐ I was surprised [at / by] the fact that …
- ☐ The most interesting finding is that …

Agreeing

- ☐ I agree with [you / your idea].
- ☐ I think so, too.
- ☐ I suppose you're right.
- ☐ I feel the same way.
- ☐ I have no objections.
- ☐ That's a good idea.

Disagreeing

- ☐ I disagree with [you / your idea].
- ☐ I don't think so.
- ☐ I have a different opinion.
- ☐ I'm against it.
- ☐ That's a good opinion, but …
- ☐ That can be true, but …

Listing / Ordering

- [ ] A is more important than B in terms of …
- [ ] A is followed by B.
- [ ] A is one of the most important items because …
- [ ] The most important point here is that …
- [ ] We should focus on importance first. Then …
- [ ] The first point is … The second point is …
- [ ] First, … [Second / Then], … [Lastly / Finally], …

Categorizing

- [ ] They can be classified into …
- [ ] A belongs to B in that …
- [ ] A is included in B
- [ ] There are [two / three / four] kinds of …

Suggesting / Evaluating

- [ ] It is suggested that …
- [ ] I would suggest that …
- [ ] It was [excellent > great > good > fair > poor > bad].
- [ ] More attention should be given to …
- [ ] You should have paid attention to …
- [ ] You had better do.

Useful Expressions for Discussions

Comparison and contrast

☐ A is the same as B.

☐ A is [similar to / like] B.

☐ Similarly, …

☐ A is different from B.

☐ In contrast, …

☐ On the other hand, …

☐ Comparing A with B, I found that …

Showing examples

☐ For [example / instance], …

☐ A is a typical example of B

☐ One example of A is … Another example of A is …

Paraphrasing

☐ In other words, …

☐ In short, …

☐ It means that …

Referring to a source

☐ According to an article, …

☐ The newspaper [said / showed / reported / described] that …

☐ A lot of studies have [proved / found / confirmed] that …

☐ As Prof. A [suggests / explains / states / claims / asserts / points out], …

Consequences

☐ As a result, …

☐ Consequently, …

☐ Therefore, …

☐ This is because …

☐ A leads to B.

Web動画のご案内 **StreamLine**

本テキストの映像は、オンラインでのストリーミング再生になります。下記
URLよりご利用ください。なお**有効期限は、はじめてログインした時点から1
年半**です。

http://st.seibido.co.jp

①

ログイン画面

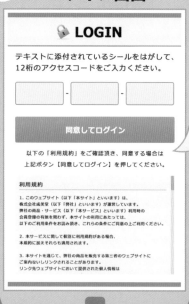

巻末に添付されている
シールをはがして、ア
クセスコードをご入
力ください。

②

メニュー画面

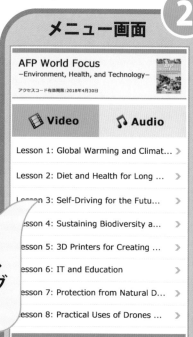

「Video」または
「Audio」を選択すると、
それぞれストリーミング
再生ができます。

③

再生画面

推奨動作環境

【PC OS】
Windows 7~ / Mac 10.8~

【Mobile OS】
iOS / Android ※Android の場合は4.x~が推奨

【Desktop ブラウザ】
Internet Explorer 9~ / Firefox / Chrome / Safari

Global Gate TESTUDY のご案内

STUDY 学習内容

教科書の学習をWeb上に再現しております。
リアルタイムで学習状況を確認することができます。

教科書タスク	TESTUDY 学習形式
Warming Up	多肢選択問題
Watching	動画再生
Vocabulary	タイピング問題
Listening Comprehension	動画再生および多肢選択問題など
Dictation	タイピング問題
Retelling	動画再生および自由記入フォーム
Discussion	自由記入フォーム
Grammar Exercise	語句整序問題
Reading	本文掲載
Vocabulary Check	タイピング問題
Reading Comprehension	自由記入フォーム
Writing	自由記入フォーム

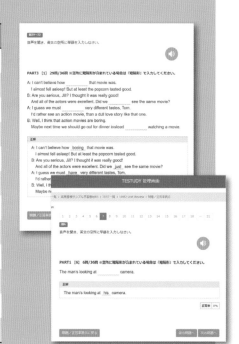

REVIEW 学習内容

授業の復習に活用することができます。

教科書タスク	TESTUDY 学習形式
Vocabulary	多肢選択問題
Tips on Listening and Speaking	音声認識学習
Dictation	タイピング問題
Grammar Exercise	語句整序問題

※教員の指示に従って学習・受験してください。　133

著 者

青田 庄真	（茨城大学 助教）
輿石 采佳	（慶應義塾大学 非常勤講師）
Bill Benfield	（株式会社成美堂）
森田 彰	（早稲田大学 教授）

TEXT PRODUCTION STAFF

edited by	編集
Takashi Kudo	工藤 隆志
Eiichi Tamura	田村 栄一
Mitsugu Shishido	宍戸 貢
Hiroshi Yoshizuka	吉塚 弘

cover design by	表紙デザイン
Nobuyoshi Fujino	藤野 伸芳

DTP by	DTP
ALIUS (Hiroyuki Kinouchi)	アリウス（木野内 宏行）

CD PRODUCTION STAFF

recorded by	吹き込み者
Dominic Allen (AmE)	ドミニク・アレン（アメリカ英語）
Howard Colefield (AmE)	ハワード・コールフィルド（アメリカ英語）
Rachel Walzer (AmE)	レイチェル・ワルザー（アメリカ英語）
Karen Headrich (AmE)	カレン・ヘドリック（アメリカ英語）

Global Gate Basic
-Video-based Four Skills Training-

2024年1月20日　初版発行
2024年2月15日　第2刷発行

著　　者	青田 庄真　輿石 采佳
	Bill Benfield　森田 彰
発 行 者	佐野 英一郎
発 行 所	株式会社 成 美 堂
	〒101-0052　東京都千代田区神田小川町3-22
	TEL 03-3291-2261　FAX 03-3293-5490
	https://www.seibido.co.jp

印刷・製本　三美印刷株式会社

ISBN 978-4-7919-7281-4　　　　　　　　　　Printed in Japan